THE MBONGI
An African Traditional Political Institution

K. Kia Bunseki FU-KIAU , Ph.D

A
Eureka
to
The African Crisis

Afrikan Djeli Publishers

ISBN-13 978-0-9798951-0-4
ISBN-10 0-9798951-0-3

Available from:

Afrikan Djeli Publishers
P.O. Box 50130
Atlanta, GA 30302-0130

www.Fukiau.com
www.AfrikanDjeli.com

TABLE OF CONTENTS

"The quality of a society and civilization [should] be measured by the respect shown to the weakest of its members"

John-Paul II

"Public knowledge and public condemnation are needed to curb those who torture or imprison or otherwise punish the innocent"

Jimmy Carter

"If a free society cannot help the many who are poor, it cannot save the few who are rich"

John F. Kennedy

"We will all be dead if the forest [the substructural ground of our system of survival] is exterminated"

Bambuti (pigmy) proverb

"Mbôngi va lwèka lwa fu kia kânda, lôko"—"A community political institution beside its system is a cancer for the community"

Kôngo proverb

INTRODUCTION

Modern Africa is often a stranger to itself. Its so-called institutions are also alien to it. The national economic disease spreading to many African states is not African in origin. It is a disease generated by alien economic systems blindly adopted or being adopted by African leaders who have never sat inside an African "Mbôngi," a truly indigenous political institution.

Modern economic Africa is rooted outside of the truly "African" Africa which is the principal reason the great majority of people throughout Africa are suffering. African leaders have a hard time setting up sound economic policy because national institutions and those to whom they are responsible are rooted in systems little known to them and to their people. Very often these institutions (schools, banks, corporations, agencies) are run from the outside world.

African leaders are accused of being incompetent by their fellow countrymen. The latter formulate interesting critiques to address those in power but, very often, these critiques ring hollow. They do not suggest what should be done. Such critiques are often without substance because they talk about the same systems about which they have only a very superficial functional and organizational knowledge. They often basically miss critical problems and issues of Africa today.

Many newly elected African leaders go to Paris, Moscow or Washington the day after their inauguration to recruit not only technicians for technical expertise, but counselors, secretaries, house girls and even crime organizers. Such behavior often proves, perhaps without their own knowledge, that such leaders themselves are hired to serve the same masters and the same political system that does not have any roots in the local cultural environment. Yet interestingly, every African waits for Western or Eastern ideological camps not only to change the hated regime of his country but also to draw critiques about the regime in power from such foreign sources—"Paris said so;" "Washington has agreed;" "Moscow may disagree"... and so on. Such phrases have become common songs and political thermometers all over Africa.

This does not mean that African people are afraid to criticize regimes in their home countries, but rather the African masses do not often have an opinion about systems which are alien to their political as well as economical concepts. (These systems are controlled by external forces which, with money, are able to destroy everything on their path). On the other hand, because the uprising of African masses and their disagreement with imposed policies have always been repressed by dictatorial forces supported by alien banks, corporations and governments; they cannot effectively criticize home policy explained to them, often in foreign languages. The gravity of the situation expressed by such powerless masses is always labelled as insignificant by powers standing behind the mass-killer-dictators in Africa, there to shift the focus of the situation away from the reality.

The African man of "Mbôngi"—the man without any value before the dollar-man of imperialism—will never live in peace in his own continent if he cannot attack and expose the source of his suffering and the type of politics which are imposed upon him. Zimbabwe would never be free today if its leaders had not returned to negotiate with the principal source of its illness, the United Kingdom of England. And the South African Black nation of Azania will never be freed as long as the oppressed population of the continent as a whole will not unite to attack the "disease" from its source, the principal investors in that part of the continent. These investors, by and large, are more racist than the apartheid system itself. Their money is arming not only the enemy of the continent but of a whole human race, the Black Race.

Masses in Africa will remain politically and economically inactive and paralysed as long as systematically teleguided or manipulated regimes remain in power in Africa. This situation does not solely paralyse the local economy but, also, industries of countries "teleguiding" this type of policy. Nations and their economic systems are no longer isolated. The era of great and small powers is over. Each nation and its economic system is no more than a stitch in a worldwide economic web. One single stitch undone can destroy the balance of the whole web framework.

The unemployment crisis that western economic systems have become victims of today is not totally a western creation of certain administrations, as it often appears in certain political milieus. Its main source is to be found in the Third World, the source of raw materials needed in industrialized high technology based nations. The Third World, unhappy with the political systems imposed upon its inhabitants by the West, is unable to produce raw materials needed in Western and Japanese industries in order to keep them running. Western and Japanese industries have had to lay off thousands of its employees because the Third World, its source of raw materials, has taken up arms to fight against social injustice and also against its oppressor at home and abroad.

I am writing this work, which is based on a traditional African political institution, not to attack a country or a particular leader of the Black continent. Nevertheless, the message of this study directs itself to every African: educator of laborer, villager or townsman, leader or follower, to inform his or her that the source of their "African disease" which causes their communities to suffer is very complex. A facet of such complexity is the concept of the political system imposed on their countries. This concept, fundamentally alien to African socio-economic concepts, is unable to respond to African basic needs and realities. The western concept of economy inherited in Africa becomes groundless when placed

ii

upon African social, cultural and economic concepts. By adopting such an economic system, African countries are clutching at a web that they must urgently untie before it is too late.

To untie "meshes" of a system is a task which requires effort and cooperation of all active forces of a nation. Africans must be ready to accept that many mistakes have already been made since the eve of the independence of the new African nations and that those mistakes more or less belong to all of them. They also recognize that to build upon "old materials" related to an earlier African reality (a concern neglected by most African modern leaders) is not a small enterprise. Such building is often a work of intuition, wisdom and great patience. Such concern does not lack opposition. An African leader today must be convinced that he is only an electron within the body of the molecular dynamic called community or society. Without this union to other electrons of the community body (its social members), the leader becomes disengaged or ungrounded and loses the role entrusted to him by the society, since his leadership is no longer a productive role in that society. If the situation reaches this level, then the leader must give up his function as "leader." Nothing is worse than to plunge the whole nation into an abyss of misery and death as a result of disunity with the people.

To be fundamentally productive or able to respond to basic social needs within an environment where the leadership is exerted, a leader must consider the monumental value of languages and cultures of local populations as the true agents of change. The total or partial abandonment of the "Kinsikandîlu"[1] in order to adopt "Kinsonsikandîlu"[2] only aggravated the situation of an ailing Africa. The African has become alienated down to the marrow of his bones by giving up his "Kinsikandîlu" (ensemble of superficially acquired values of alien cultures). No one in today's Africa seems to be pleased with the specificities of his origin or with the modern condition brought about through the process of colonization. The African's hatred toward his own culture is also a result of the "Kinsonsikandîlu," the borrowing of everything in which the African has voluntarily or involuntarily been imprisoned. As a consequence, he has become the "missionary" of his master's culture.

As the source of all African crisis, the African intellectual must learn to appreciate and develop his ethnic pride within the national framework of which his ethnic "tribalic state" is only a part. Such pride can help form a united modern African nation where the "Kinsikandîlu" (Ensemble of African cultural values) can allow every citizen to enjoy the rights of African citizenship.

Africa today is a limping continent because its leadership is not grounded in people's cultural, political and economic concepts. Great projects and investments undertaken by African leaders and their alien rtners do not have any link of interest in responding to the basic needs of African masses. This modern African leadership forgets that these masses are that force which makes the history of nations and changes the conditions of life: the farmer, fisher, blacksmith, weaver, artist, healer, educator, etc. etc.

A good leader becomes a spark and driving force within the community for the community. Such a leader stems from people in their milieu, from their practices, through their aspirations, in their beliefs, from their concepts. No one can demand his own leadership and no one can impose it because "N'lèmbo kasôngwanga," it should be an unanimous choice of the masses.

Because we are addressing the masses and the leaders who must make of Africa a land of prosperity, plenty, and future, and because our African responsibility is to both Africa and the world, I wish this study (originally written in Kikôngo language under the title *Mbôngi a Bakulu: 'Ya-Do' Mu Lubângamu Lw'Afelika*) to be next published, jointly, in French and Kikôngo. This is to be done for the simple reason that French is the language of the elite (the ruling class) of our nation, Zaire; and the original text of Kikôngo since the terminologies related to the instituion "Mbôngi" (used in this study to define the concept Bântu of Mbôngi) reflect the cultural region of Kôngo people where the language is spoken (Angola, Cabinda, Congo, and Zaire). With this multilingual* seal, the study bears the character of an international passport, though it can reach a large audience in Africa and elsewhere.

The study itself discusses traditional African practices of administrative politics within a rural, traditional African community. It attempts to show how these practices can be useful in a modern African society. I am convinced that what succeeds in politics, at a local level of organization, can also succeed at a national level of administration.

The modern Africa suffers because many want to imitate East and West. This is to be what Africa is not. Its own leaders forget that "Kânda ka ditûngwanga va lwèka lwa fu kia nsi ko" (the society/community is not built beside its own social system). Many African leaders make very little effort to try to understand traditional African systems which, positively united, permitted the functioning of the tribal states which flourished all over Africa prior to pre-colonial time and which continue to maintain the powerful, united, active and uncorruptible political, administrative, social, and economic organization of our "Makânda," the "tribalic" communities of our villages. Why have the political and administrative organizations of these lower entities (the almost totally incorruptible institutions of our societies) not attracted the attention of

---

* We also intend to translate the study into *Kiswahili, Tshiluba* and *Lingala.*

iv

African authorities if such authorities dream of a powerful and prosperous modern Africa? Should not these regional entities of traditional African political systems give birth to new political, administrative and economic patterns that could help build the African Africa of tomorrow? An Africa removed from these local cultural substructures will be weak, poor, corruptible, divided and politically impossible to lead from afar as well as at home. It will be a perpetually rebelling Africa.

At the village level, our African communities are politically and administratively better organized than many national African governments—many for the simple reason that in rural communities, with their collective principles and politico-administrative concepts, view politics as an art. The concern is of everybody, in the community, by the community and for the community. "Once the community policy is decided," say the Kôngo, "the responsibility to carry out that policy is entrusted to the 'Nzônzi' who has to talk in the name of the community and of its members"—Kinzônzi bu kimèni dèduswa kwa mfûndu za kânda, yeko mu tèndula kio kiyekulwanga kwa nzônzi mu vova mu nkûmba a kânda ye bièla biândi.

The modern African political leader no longer has such a political concept. His irresponsibility has become the principal cause of the economic "disease" so that the entire continent suffers. He has made himself a leader for life thanks to weapons provided to him by his masters and in order to maintain his "mandateless" regime he, at once, legalizes and institutionalizes the corruption with the money provided him by his supporters—the hunters of raw materials. The rest takes its course freely: jailing, moral decline, human rights violations, poverty, insignificant penalties, famine, embezzlements, bloody violence, bankruptcy, neocolonization.

Contrary to modern Africa, the African tradition calls for a praising of the chief during his mandate, while assaulting songs are addressed as a stimulus to his or her leadership. The dictum is never to worship him, his actions or what he promises to do. Today we are witnessing manifestations throughout Africa which sing not of the deeds of leaders but of empty and untruthful promises. These modern songs mash the words of chiefs instead of bringing them advice and constructive criticism. And our leaders and their followers will say that they are making a revolution. This is not a revolution, just a shift in challenges to leaders. Such a shift will, in the end, harvest nothing but piles of debt files from all over the world.

The time has come for African people to learn that all revolution that is busy in singing and dancing is a revolution that corrupts, alienates and kills active forces of a nation whatever its potential human and natural resources may be. After that revolution of "cicadas," only ruins and confusions will exist.

Because of the danger such a revolution presents, African traditional wisdom puts every leader on his guard in order not to be duped into such a revolution or be a leader that can be flattered by the sound of drums while one is oneself an empty barrel. "Mfumu matu; kavwa n'nwa ko" (a chief is a listener, he is without a mouth) says a Kôngo proverb.

The African chief has always been a listener, an "ears' owner," i.e. a learner all the time he is a chief. This is to allow him to clearly see questions of general and urgent interest arising throughout the community. Many questions could, it mismanaged, lead to a break of the "Nîngunu a n'singa dikânda" (the physical and spiritual union of the community) that should be maintained the stretched. The esoteric expression above signifies the perpetual referral of the present community to its past (historico-cultural experience) in order to shape its future. A leader who is himself busy with the cicada-like revolution, always animation and singing, has no time to listen or to understand social problems and their impact as to what building a nation is concerned.

If Africa was a world of listening chiefs, "chiefs without mouth," why then, one may ask, do its modern chiefs talk so much like empty barrels and do almost nothing? Do they fear hearing from the people the truth of their wrong-doing? Why should they fear critiques? Are they not African chiefs, "the ears' owners"? Does not our African wisdom tell us that a leader is a target for all kinds of assaults? Why proclaim oneself an African leader if one cannot bear those African qualities of leadership: Listen more and talk less? Why not learn to feel radiations that express people's fundamental and urgent needs? Why should one stay in power for more than one mandate (which is the most important step in any political system) if one's policy was detrimental to the people—one's constituency? Is it not a national shame for an unwanted leader to stay in power when one knows pertinently that one's work suffers total destruction on the eve or the next day of one's death or withdrawal from power?

It seems, unfortunately, that politics for African leaders is the art of distributing precious minerals as well as selling out the political and human rights of African citizens. Such a view, though widespread among African leaders, is wrong and should be eradicated as soon as possible. Because of this "non-sense" behavior on the part of African leaders, there is a need to study and to understand African traditional political institutions of the past as they are lived in rural community. These institutions will teach them how a leader takes care of "mbôngo a kânda" (the community material goods/the commonwealth of the community) in order to understand how to take care of common wealth or public property.

The modern political Africa needs a change. This change, we are sure, cannot come about unless African leaders turn themselves to listen to the cries of their people. With such a willingness, we can change the conditions of life which African countries and their masses are driven into.

One of the most important steps that a modern African leader can make to save his people from the chaos that even he, perhaps, is the creator of, is to put on "truck" a government of the type Mbôngi," as we will see later on, for an incorruptible African economic policy. This is a type of government that will be grounded neither on capitalistic nor communalistic structures. It will be deep-rooted into the local "Kisinsi" (systems) expressed by the local social, cultural, political, religious, economic, linguistic, and philosophic practices of African local realities. The access to this step, we are convinced, will permit all sons and daughters of African nations at all levels of sensibilities to develop great hopes for African needs as well as the world's.[3]

Past radiations of African cultures and civilizations are sensitizing African people to the kinds of organizations African societies need with their politico-economic structures. The understanding of these traditional civilization can enable societies to respond adequately to their presently urgent needs as the only way to warrant their future throughout "N'kîngu mia dingo-dingo," the vital principles of life and change.

Made sensitive by those spiritual and cultural radiations of our African heritage "rolled" in the spiral hole of the past for immediate and mediate needs, I decided to write this message to help, in some manner, those who hold in their hands the key of the African's future. These key-holders, African leaders, politicians and scholars, must consider this message if they wish to save the ailing Black continent and the people they are dragging into the present course of misery and death. This safety would be impossible in Africa unless its present leaders open the door not only for self-criticism but for public critiques as well through press and mass-media.

Modern African leaders, in as well as outside the continent, must become aware of socio-cultural and frontier realities of the countries under their leadership. Considering their extent, certain of these countries can be taken as simple American counties[4] while others constitute an ensemble of states within states with enormous cultural differences. One can clearly see that colonial conventional boundaries inherited by the Third World Nations (Africa in particular) do not respond to socio-cultural or even geographic realities. It is, in my point of view, upon the basis of these social and cultural overlapping African realities that an African continental diplomcy of "good neighborhood" must be founded. The inherited boundaries of the colonial era should not destroy social, cultural and full-blooded links that naturally unite people of one area of a country to those of other countries within the ancient bounding lines of their tribal or ethnic states.

African leaders must, in other words, understand that modern African nations are made up of overlapping rings of ethnic states which cover over our modern national frontiers inherited from the colonization

Fig. 1: African modern states are made up of colonially "broken rings" of ethnic kingdoms and empires which "touch" beyond their national frontiers. The map above shows the modern republic of Angola on certain of those ancient, African traditional states from which Angola owes its people. These people are ethnic groups split between Congo (1), Zaire (2), Zambia (3), and Namibia (4).

period. This situation represents one of the greatest and most sensitive problems that African has inherited from its masters (fig. 1) but, on the other side, this situation is the ground upon which African policy of neighborhood can be built. Africans must be interested in these basically human and spiritual questions that unite their people and their cultures beyond modern national frontiers. Imprudence to this basic concern can only perpetuate national political and economic insecurity.

It is possible to reduce the intellectual effort of a lefthanded child while imposing him, whether he likes it or not, the use of his right hand. What can happen in the mind of a child forced to write only with his right hand (when his driving manual power is concentrated at his left hand) can also happen to the "heart" of a nation to which one imposes an alien political or economic system which may not have any root/foundation in the "heart" of that particular nation, i.e. its basic system of social, philosophical, and human values. "Fu va lwèka lwa kânda, lôdo" (A political system beside community social realities is a cancer), a Kôngo proverb says. And it seems that most African political systems have become carcinogenic today because most of them have been built beside the African local systems and far from their social and economic realities.

Human beings in all societies, developed or non developed, are aware that there are certain cultural or human links which are very hard to break, even through political means. USA frontiers, for example, will almost always remain open to Anglo-Saxons living in Canada who are not USA citizens: "Canadian citizens and British subjects domiciled in Canada entering for business or pleasure for a period of six months or less are not required to present passports or visas of any kind," states R. McNalley.[5] Where deep and natural relationships exist, all political, diplomatic and legal conditions are often flexible.

We hope that, with these words of introduction for our readers, *The Mbôngi: An 'Eureka' To African Crisis* will stir the interest of African intellectuals and official leaders who must lay the foundation of the African policy and its orientation. Such leaders and intellectuals have the chance to save the perishing African race in continental Africa and elsewhere in the world where its survival is threatened.

K. Kia Bunseki, FU-KIAU
J.P. Cambridge, 1981.

CHAPTER I
MBONGI

The "Mbôngi" is a common "shelter" of very simplistic architecture that one finds in the middle of almost every village in the Bântu countries in general and in Kôngo region in particular. The construction is the physical living symbol of one of the most powerful and most important African traditional political institutions. Its terminology varies from one Bântu sub-cultural region to another. The Mbôngi is generally called *Lubanza* among the Luba, *Baraza* among the Swahili, and *Mbôngi* among the Kôngo people. This study of Mbôngi as an African traditional political institution is based on the Kôngo cultural region comprising the North of Angola, the Cabinda, the South of the Congo and the South-West of Zaire.

Knowing the root of the word Mbôngi[6] should be the first step for anyone willing to understand such a concept beyond that "terminology" according to the "Kibântu" (Bântu philosophy) and the socio-economic systems that that philosophy transfers. Each Bântu cultural region has its own definition and usage of the term "Mbôngi." The definition which concerns us here is taken from the Kôngo cultural region which extends from the North of the Angolan Popular Republic, the South-West of Zaire, Cabinda, and the Congolese Popular Republic.

In this central-west African culture, the term Mbôngi and the concept it expresses are derived from the verbal root *"Bônga."* The latter signifies "to take, to seize, to accept, to make one's possession, to own." Contextually one can "Bônga mbebe/yeko, zitu, mpasi, nzèngolo, mâmbu evo mfuka" (take a responsibility, a burden, a pain, a decision, risks, a debt). "Bônga Yeko " taking a Responsibility, Y/R, is comparing oneself to the weight of the Responsibility to be taken but, also, deciding if one is able to head the "kimfumu kia Mbôngi," the leadership of the Mbôngi, the most important political institution present in every rural Bântu traditional community. This is to become responsible for it and becomes a lifter of all oppressing yokes borne by the community. "Bônga Yeko," to take a Responsibility, is supposed to lighten the weight of social and economic problems of the community and relieve its members. It is finding a uniform and acceptable answer for whoever bore the weight of the burden. It is heading or directing that responsibility in private as well as in public.

From the root "Bônga," to take, many other important terminologies are derived which explain the Bântu social organization of the community life:

Bônga—to take, to possess, to bear, to accept with will of heading

Bôngi or M'bôngi—the one who takes (responsibilities, etc.)

Bôngo or Bôngolo—tool/instrument used to take; a model, form, what is taken; medicinal plant

Bôngwa—to be taken; what is taken; data; model

Kimbôngi—the teaching of and about Mbôngi; right of Mbôngi

Kimfumu-mbôngi—responsibility and leadership of the "Mfumu-mbôngi"

Lubôngo—sing. of "Mbôngo" (see Mbôngo)

Mbônga—manner of taking or handling (responsibility, leadership)

Mbôngi—public-council-house; institution of debates and of conceptualization, the community parliament; the popular court of justice among African people; source, origin, fireplace

M'bôngi—the one who takes or causes

Mbôngo—pl. of "Lubôngo;" "object" used to "take" (= exchange) goods, etc., money, goods, produce, income; clothes

M'bôngo (bôngo)—form, model; manner of taking something

Me Mbôngi—head of Mbôngi

Mfumu-mbôngi—head/leader of Mbôngi, president of Mbôngi

Because of the importance of the term's role among members of the community, the Mbôngi is known under diverse names among the Kôngo people: *Mbôngi, Boko, Yèmba, Lusânga, Kiôto*. The concept Bântu of Mbôngi is also linked to terminologies given to this institution according to theoretical and proverbal ideas related to it and its function as a political institution.

Through theories and proverbs related to Mbôngi terminologies we can clearly detect the functions and values of the institution "Mbôngi" to the Bântu social and political organization (in African traditional community) among the people living south of the Saharian belt. We will group a few proverbs around each central term of Mbôngi related to it in Kikôngo, the original language of the study, with their translation in English.

1. Central term "mbôngi."

1.1. Mbôngi wabônga mâmbu ma kânda (finangani kiândi) Mbôngi wabônga ntântani za kânda.

The mbôngi "takes" (discusses) all problems of the community (variant). It is the community mbôngi that "takes" social conflicts in the community.

1.2. Mbôngi walûnda mbôngo a kânda.

The Mbôngi takes care of human as well as material goods of the community.

1.3. Nsusu ambakala kubila ku mbôngi.

A true rooster in the community can only crow in the Mbôngi.

1.4. Zakala va kikulu kia mbôngi mbo' wata kikulu kia kânda.

Sit on the Mbôngi's stool (that transfers history) and you will be able to tell the history of the community.

1.5. Mbôngi mbôngo a kânda.

The Mbôngi does what is good for the community (lit. The Mbôngi is the source of community wealth / knowledge)

1.6. Mâmbu ma kânda kimbilu ku mbôngi.

All problems in the community run / go towards Mbôngi.

1.7. Kimbilu ku mbôngi lusunga.

Any political conflict, in the Mbôngi, is caused by the direction shift of leadership.

1.8. Mbôngi yakôndwa ntungasani; (nga) ka nkote ko zo e?

A Mbôngi where self-criticism is not tolerated is a strange and an inconceivable political institution.

1.9. Mbôngi bôngo kia nsi ye kânda.

The Mbôngi is, by excellency, the "medicine" of a country and its communities.

1.10. Wayina, yinina ku mbôngi.

Individual dissatisfaction must be expressed in the Mbôngi (it should not be shown outside of it).

1.11. Kinzônzi katoma, ku mbôngi; kabiya mpe, ku mbôngi.

All polities, good or bad, should be discussed (openly) in the Mbôngi, the public-council-house.

1.12. Wagâmbula mbôngi, vo k'u zoba ko, kânda lwêngisi.

Do you create (found) your own Mbôngi? If you do without being "lunatic," you are warning the community government and its leadership.

1.13. Luyâlu mu kânda, dîmbu mbôngi.

The Mbôngi is the physical symbol of the community government.

1.14. Mbôngi is siku dia kânda (fin. kiândi) Mbôngi wasikidisa kânda.

The Mbôngi is the stand/standarizer of the community life style (var.) It is the Mbôngi that regularizes or stabilizes the community life style.

1.15. Mfûndu za mbôngi (wafundumuna mâmbu ye bibila mu kânda) ka zisûmbwanga ko.

The commissions of the Mbôngi (which "dig up"/reveal social dealings and conflicts) are incorruptible.

1.16. Wabulwa mèso zakala ĝa mbôngi.

To have one's eyes opened (towards secrecy of life), one has to sit in the Mbôngi assemblies.

1.17. Kânda dianene mbôngi ubûndisanga dio.

A large community founds its unity on the ground of the Mbôngi, its parliament, the public-council-house—(Political and economic unity in the middle of cultural, social and philosophical diversity unites diverse social and ethnic groups in great, strong and powerful entities).

1.18. Mbông'i didi dia kânda.

The Mbôngi is the center (thinktank) of the community.

1.19. Kânda diakôndwa mbôngi difwîdi (diswâsani) Kânda diakôndwa mbôngi dia bilauki.

The community without the institution Mbôngi—when it used to have one—dies (var.) The community without Mbôngi belongs to the insame (madmen).

1.20. Mbông'i longokolo kia fu kia nsi

The Mbôngi is the school that teaches/instructs about the system (custom) of the community/country.

1.21. Mbông'i n'tim'a kânda ku nseke.

The Mbôngi is the heart of the living community (in the upper or physical world).

2. Central term "boko."

This second group comprises proverbs centered around the term Boko whose root, bokula related to bôka, signifies "to break/to cut" in the sense of deciding and solving problems.

2.1. Mbil'a boko ni beto kulu.

The call of boko belongs to all of us.

2.2. Boko dia n'kuyu na' wayena dio.

Who sees the boko of N'kuyu, the stunted (ill-thriven) ancestor [where one talks of good things about a deviant ancestor]?

2.3. Boko wabôka mu kânda.

It is the boko that calls up everything in the community.

2.4. Boko wabokula mâmbu mu (ma) kânda.

It is the boko that "breaks" (solves) the social problems within the community.

2.5. Boko wabôkila tèmbo mu kânda.

It is also in the boko that "storms" (troubles) are called in the community.

2.6. Boko wakônga makânda.

It is the boko that gathers communities (for alliances and mutual interests).

2.7. Boko ka ditûngwanga ku lutèngo ko.

The boko is not built "aside" (of the physical and spiritual community).

2.8. Boko ka ditûngwanga va lwèka lwa *fu* kia nsi ko.

The boko is not found beside the *system* of the community/country.

2.9. Boko n'tâmbu.

The boko is a trap.

2.10. Wafûngila boko vengamane.

You will see yourself deviating if you do not go along with the boko, its political and philosophical outline.

2.11. Mfûndu za boko ka zisômpolongo zu ko.

Secrets of boko are not discussed in a "borrowed" language [that betrays the boko/mbôngi and its system].

3. Central term "yèmba."

The central term of this group, "Yèmba," signifies at once verandah and wing whose role is to cover in order to protect. Through the Mbôngi government community members are not only covered but protected as well. Here follow a few proverbs related to the term:

3.1. Mbil'a yêmba vo ka ya dia ko, ya mâmbu.

The call of yèmba, if not for some common meal, concerns a community problem.

3.2. Yèmba wayembamana   mâmbu ma kânda (dis.) Yèmba wayembamana kânda.

It is the yèmba that covers up community problems (var.) It is the yèmba that covers/protects the community.

3.3. Yèmba wayembika n'tâmbu mia kânda.

It is the yèmba that installs community traps (seeks ways and means to solve community problems).

3.4. Yèmba wanikuna mayèmbo ma kânda.

It is the yèmba that puts all community human resources (together) in motion—Lit. shakes community forces.

3.5. Yèmba diakônga bilèsi mu kânda.

It is the yèmba that calls up the community youth (for initiation draft).

3.6. Sâna mu kânda yèmba usânsanga bio.

It is the yèmba that takes care of orphans in the community.

3.7. Yèmba wayèmba mâmbu (mu diâmbu dia kânda).

The yèmba spies (for the community).

3.8. Ku yèmba ka kukèmbwanga ko.

There is no flirting with yèmba.

4. Central term "lusânga."»

Lusânga, the central term of this group, is a derivative of the root verb "sânga." This latter means "to mix," "to put together," "to assemble." Lusânga in this sense is an institution that gathers not only community members but the human experience of communities as well. Here are a few proverbs related to the term "lusânga:"

4.1. Lusânga wasangumuna mayenda mu kânda.

It is the lusânga that reviews and revives everything that goes within the community.

4.2. Lusânga walûnda kîdidi (kinenga) kia kânda.

It is the lusânga that keeps the community's warmth (harmony/balance).

4.3. Lusânga wasangumukina (telemana) kânda.

It is the lusânga that stands straight up to defend the community (against its foes) or to blame it (in its own wrong doing).

4.4. Lusânga wasengumuna nsângu za kânda.

It is the lusânga (sole) that reveals community's (classified) news/information (to its members).

4.5. Luseke-seke lwa lusânga, lusunga lwa kânda.

The community's warmth (balance/harmony) depends upon its (political) direction.

4.6. Mbil'a lusânga ni muna bôkele yo.

The call of lusânga depends on he who "formulates" it.

4.7. Kikesa kia makesa nkuma za lusânga utûnganga kio.

It is the experience transferred by lusânga that builds the (community) military courage.

5. Central term "Kiôto."

The central term in this group, Kiôko, signifies literally "inhalation." In this sense the Mbôngi in a community, its government, is a political, social and spiritual or psychological "cure." Below a few proverbs related to kiôto or kiôko, the fifth terminology related to Mbôngi:

5.1. Nsângu za kânda ku kiôto ziyadulwanga (tewulwanga).

Community news is told in the kiôto.

5.2. Kiôto, kiôto, kia kânda.

The kiôto is an inhalation inside the community.

Meals in the kiôto do not come by themselves, they are brought (by its members)—[A policy that feeds its people or pretends to develop the nation on the ground of alien gifts is carcinogenic.]

5.4. Kiôto, kikulu mu kânda (kônso-kônso kavwânda kwândi).

The kiôto house is like a stool in the community (each of its members has the right to sit on it in order to be sensibilized by the past experience and foster the present and the future.)

---

*Lusânga is also known as *Lukânga/Lukângala*, from *kânga* (to tie/tighten), a fire that unites and ties together community members in an unbroken circle around the "warming force/energy" of the community lukânga.

5.5. Ma ku kiôto matûnga' kânda.
What is taught in the kiôto builds the community.
5.6. Kwena kiôto kwena lusikudusü.
Where there is kiôto, there is a constitution.
5.7. Mayenda ye nzo mankaka; ma kiôto, ma kiôto (dis.) Ma nzo, ma nzo; ma kiôto, ma kiôto.
What goes with a household is different from what goes with the community kiôto (var.) What belongs to the household goes with the household; that of the kiôto with the kiôto.
5.8. Kièlo kia kiôto buna kiazibuka.
The door of the kiôto is always open (to everybody).
5.9. Vwânda ku kiôto kuyalwa nkuma ye ngana z'ekulu ye nkudulu.
Sit in the kiôto where experience and proverbs on history (tradition) and knowledge on development are transferred.

Such theories and proverbs related to the term Mbôngi and its variants give us a clear idea about the function, the value and the definition of Mbôngi the key word in this study.

For those belonging to the "Kibântu," the Bântu philosophical system, including the Fang, Kôngo, Luba, Bemba, Sona, Mbûndu, Zulu, Xosa, etc., the Mbôngi still is the highest and most important political institution of the community today, constituting everything for the community. It is the institution Mbôngi that "constitutes" the community and which leads and protects its constitution. Under this "constitution" the community decrees, i.e. makes community or national laws (N'siku) for the community. It determines community members' responsibilities and their rights (N'swa) according to the community's unwritten constitution. In other words, we can say that Mbôngi, for the Bantu people, is the first and the only institution that had and still has the real power in modern Africa of each regional system concerning the political art of leading people according to their fundamental African oral constitutions. Aside from the Mbôngi, there is no other institution which had this broad responsibility in structural or administrative policy within the community as well as within the continent as a whole.

Contrary to what usually goes on in the gatherings of the townsmen (where conversations on beer, soccer, salary increases, mistresses, and up to date music prevail), problems and issues related to social, political and economic basic needs of the community and its members occupy the time of Mbôngi meetings. Here the sense and the need for planning, democracy and self-criticism are very noticeable. This is not the case in cities where the Mbôngi has defaulted. And, interestingly enough, it seems that in the process of modern African nation-building, leaders from cultural regions where the concept of Mbôngi and its role were clearly defined are more cooperative and more open to critiques and to the modern concept of democracy than those from areas where the Mbôngi did not exist or where its role was vaguely defined.

Mbôngi is not only a politico-educational institution; it is also a strong and lovely model of a common household. It is the "shaper" of the community leadership of the African traditional life. Its lack is destructive to the community and to its balance, cfr. "Kânda diakôndwa mbôngi difwîdi" (A community without the institution Mbôngi is subject to death) and the variant, "Kânda diakôndwa mbôngi dia bilauki" (A community without Mbôngi belongs to insane/madmen, proverb 1.19).

All issues of public interest, be they social, political or economic, must openly and publicly be discussed in public institutions teaches the Bântu traditional political wisdom of Mbôngi.

When a community/society or a nation can no longer make decisions in the public interest with its public institutions (such as Mbôngi among the Bântu people), the future of such a nation becomes frightening. This is the case for many young African nations because their rulers have made public problems an affair of their "clan." These rulers, as a consequence, hate and avoid all elements of growth: truth and critiques from their own people. The fear of truth and critiques among African leaders is the principal cause of economic crisis, starvation and of death today in Africa. This situation will change only if one can seriously learn the art of ruling or managing people from the substructures of their African traditional political institutions such as the Mbôngi. From this basis, African people can build modern and solid African institutions of law and social justice.

It is a great mistake not to consider foundations of such traditional political institutions and the cultural heritage that has accumulated in people's minds and cultures in modern Africa. Due to their advanced technology and their innumerable powerful weapons, agents of imperialism have partially succeeded in oppressing the "Kisinsi," local systems, and have built through violent means new governments based on alien political and economic systems—The better to watch over the natives and their activities in order to prevent any revolt or need of reestablishing their "Kisinsi," the banned local system. Everything that is "root" and "force" to Mwisinsi, the indigenous, has been categorically prohibited by agents of the new system. Local institutions of initiation were substituted by a new system of education. African languages were banished from schools because they were not "scientific;" local systems of economy and their practices were considered insane. The good land that produced food to nourish community members and nations was seized for animal and coffee production (products of exportation) instead of being used for growing grains which the human being requires for survival—as a consequence the whole of Africa is starving today.

Because of his ignorance of the local political system and due to his cultural arrogance, the colonialist imposed an individual, the watchdog to the Kânda (the local community), to become a spokesperson for agents of exploitation. This "go-between" individual in between the colonial government and the local government at the village level is called "Dûki," from the French, "duc." But very interestingly, this "duc" was never called in the Kôngo milieu "Duc of Mbôngi" or "Duc of Kânda." Since the Mbôngi was itself the local government which was systematically ignored by the agents of imperialism, the go-between individual was always known as "The duc of the village" by the local system which clearly proves that this individual did not have his hands on the "heart" of the local system. Was this a trick? No, it was not. People were aware that his official title was "aside" the local political system. The community knew that he was a "bought" individual who had to play the role of "Kinsekwa-mu-nzèmba," a double agent. The colonial government had ignored the principal role of Mbôngi and its presence in the middle section of each village. The only Mbôngi this government knew was the "physical Mbôngi" as "Lukângala" (a place to warm oneself) and that was it.

As a solid political institution in a society of non-written literacy, the Mbôngi was unknown to colonial imperialism and its agents, be they civil or military, laymen or religious. Many political plots against agents of colonization were organized from the inside of this solid African institution, the Mbôngi, be it Mbôngi a Kânda (Community Mbôngi) or Mbôngi a Zûnga (Regional Mbôngi), known also as Zându (market). This was the case during the period of portage and hammock. Many colonial agents or their family members and goods as well as documents were sunk into rivers as means of resistance laid by Mbôngi strategies to fight against portage and against colonialism.

The colonial government survived under a haze before the "Kisinsi," the local system, and its political organization. African authorities today are in the same situation before their own "Kisinsi" because they are leading their nations while standing afar from their own African systems in matter of politics, economy and management as well. Administrative structures and organization introduced by the same colonial government that Africa disqualified as obstacles to the well-being of its populations and to its development became, to the eyes of the leaders of free Africa, the basis that is laying all administrative policy of modern independent Africa. Why, then, did one first chase the colonialist if his policy and his system of economy were later to be so perfectly duplicated after he is gone? Did African politicians really know why and what their masses and themselves were fighting for and against? Such a behavior is a great mistake on the part of African people; a mistake due to ignorance and our own hatred of ourselves, and resentment against politico-economic concepts and cultures generated by our own African systems.

Uprisings of African masses that we are witnessing throughout the whole African continent are consequences of this African attitude towards their own concepts and their cultures. And no one is asking why. Our African "Kisinsi" is clear about this question: Any political conflict (crisis) in the Mbôngi system is only a produce of the directional shift of its leadership (proverb 1.7). People do not want any more supporting governments that plan everything on the basis of "outside gifts" cfr. proverb 5.3: A policy that feeds its people or pretends to develop the nation on the ground of alien gifts is carcinogenic.

A disorder or a revolt does not occur in the Mbôngi if this latter is under the supervision and direction of those leaders who possess authority deep-rooted within the people's common consent according to their concepts and their cultural values. These are concepts and values based upon their own economic systems and upon their constitutions, written or not. It is here that the African modern "Kinzônzi" (the art of dealing with public matters/politics) should find its true source of inspiration and of revival.

Because we will frequently come back to the term Kinzônzi in this study, we must define it according to its use in the Bantu cultures, especially among the Kôngo, before our discussion continues.

Among the Bântu, "Kinzônzi," especially in central-west Africa, is a branch of knowledge (science), an art. As a branch of knowledge, the Kinzônzi teaches administrative, organizational, judiciary, clinical and diplomatic wisdom. As an art, it teaches and initiates in techniques and wisdom of "words" (speeches) and of eloquence (rhetoric) within the community. Africanists have never had a deep interest in Kinzônzi, a key subject to all Bântu political philosophy. We will later come back to this particular point.

Tension, intimidation, violence and wars exist anywhere where there are "westernized" intellectuals in Africa, primarily in large cities which are the centers of exploiting forces. In contrast, the villager community, in spite of authorities' repression and their violent intimidation continues to keep its security and that of its members in deep rural milieus. Notwithstanding this difference between townsman behavior and that of the hinterlandsman (the "man of the bush," as he is labbelled in cities), no intellectual asks himself why the villager is different in his social organization compared to the townsman, the self-labelled "civilized African."

The simplest answer to the question is that the townsman, in all his organizations, lives without any solid system in his mind. On the contrary, the villager or the "bushman" (or "le broussard" as he is called by his fellow countrymen of cities), in spite of his lack of political power at the national level, is deep-rooted in a solid system that places his community and himself master. It is the system taught and transferred in the most respected African political institution, the community Mbôngi.

This system is the "Fu-Kia-Nsi" or "Kisinsi" (the system or custom of the country). This Kisinsi has an expression or a language of its own that allows it to be transferred to its people where the following say "Ma ku Mbôngi ka matômbulwanga zu ko" (The Mbôngi does not borrow dialects in order to discuss its political matters or to educate its members). The Kisinsi has a culture also—the culture of the people involved. It has a tradition lived by its people and by its peoples' ancestors. It is a system that lives and circulates inside every villager's blood. It is the fundamental and undeniable African self—the self that feels and dreams Africa in African expressions with African words.

Because of the "Kisinsi" taught by the Mbôngi constitution, wars, thefts, illicit salaries, plots, gunning and kidnapping (labels of westernized cities) swifly leave communities and their members who have to learn to live "Ku nsia ntungasani" (under sincere public self-criticism.) The townsman does not live such a life because he is not governed by a system taught by a Mbôngi constitution but by systems whose roles and orders are given in a language unknown by him. It is in this situation that the townsman of lower class becomes the direct prey to exploitation by the ruling class and its neo-colonial masters.

Where there is no institution of the Mbôngi type that should be taking the responsibility (bônga yeko/mbebe) of solving problems raised in society, all kinds of hurts appear, psychological as well as physical. The African political organization of its economy today does not favor proper forms of development because there is a total absence of Mbôngi, a solid institution which is able to develop in national youth the spirit of the true "Kisinsi," as well as a nationally oriented policy based upon local economic concepts.

Very few citizens in Black Africa know how their country is economically or even politically organized because their modern constitutions were first of all written by foreigners in foreign languages known by a very minor fraction of corrupted individuals. This signifies that the great majority of the African population knows nothing about their so called national constitutions or their rights of citizenship. They are more "foreign" than foreigners living in their countries—worse than foreign in certain countries since publications in local languages have been banned in order to dupe the masses.

The situation is totally different in the case of the village community members concerning "Kisinsi." Each community member knows the structure and the organization of his community in spite of its lacking a written constitution. Each member knows his rights and his responsibilities before the community and knows this according to traditional unwritten constitutions preserved by the teaching of Mbôngi. Everybody has a sufficient knowledge of the system and of the community constitution because each villager has the right to sit on the "Kikulu" (lit. the seat that transfers the past), the stool of Mbôngi, in order to "Kula" (to grow), i.e. to make one's own history through the culture and the language. This, in turn allows the development of deep insight of the "Kisinsi" taught by the local constitutional system.

We have defined, above, the Mbôngi as an institution of great importance in the framework of political and administrative organization among the Bântu. Let us now examine the structure of this institution, its organizational and administrative policy.

CHAPTER II
MBONGI AS A POLITICAL INSTITUTION

The art of leading or guiding community policy is not a new skill to indigenous Africa. Tradition as well as documents of the pre-colonial and colonial era widely confirm the African leadership of the past. It is only modern rulers of Africa who are alien to their own African systems of political and economic thought. And it is here that the modern African crisis has initiated its unthinkable destruction. Many such rulers are specialized in a variety of fields which do not have any foundation in the African milieu. They want willy-nilly to impose a strange adopted technocracy in Africa without any African basis of orientation. In African eyes, such specialists will continue hanging in the air with all their "specialities," high above the Atlantic Ocean between Africa and the West unless they adapt their specialities to African reality—a continent of fundamentally federated communities.

Each Bântu society had, as one can still see it today, an institution similar to the Mbôngi among the Kôngo, in order to organize and to guide the policy of the community. This Mbôngi is so simple in its physical architecture that no attempt can be made to minimize the monumental value of the concept it describes and symbolizes for each African community and its social life. The Mbôngi is the simplest of all constructions of a village community in order to camouflage its powerful political role during the colonial epoch—yet we are convinced this will change with time. The Mbôngi generally occupies the center of the village or of the community. Its position confirms the community teaching about the place this institution occupies within the physical structure of the community as well as in the mind of its members, cfr: "The boko is not founded beside the system of the community" (proverb 2.8) and "The boko is not built aside [of the village/community]" (proverb 2.7).

According to African traditional thought, the physical institution of Mbôngi must be erected in the middle of the central portion of the physical community, the village; cfr to "The Mbôngi is the center of the community" (proverb 1.18). This is where the community system and its constitution operate and only there will the Mbôngi be respected by the community for which it has to work. We must also say something at this point about the Mbôngi position within the community in relation to the arrival of Western church agents, the missionaries, in Africa.

Upon his arrival, the missionary of the western religion destroyed the Mbôngi by violence and built upon this central position of the community's "physical universe" his "God's house" or temple. In less hostile milieus, the missionary opted to build next to the Mbôngi in order to prevent sitting inside the Mbôngi during the time of his own ceremonial practices. With the increase of torture through colonial oppression, later natives discovered and saw this new western institution, a very well built "Mbôngi," as a new form of their own Mbôngi. Nobody owned this new "Mbôngi," and nobody stayed within it. The sole difference between the old and new Mbôngi was that inside the "church" people are like "insane" and talked to an unseen "being" called "Father." But in the case of Mbôngi, people went there to talk and discuss the problems of the community, their own problems, in order to find acceptable solutions by themselves and for themselves. For African people sitting inside, the new Mbôngi (temple/cathedral) was a pure practice of magic. With colonial pressure they were pushed towards the umbrella of this new Mbôngi to discover its mysteries and its magic. Under this umbrella they began to organize their political subversions against the colonial oppression.

In the case of Zaire (openly since 1906) as soon as people learned that their country was at stake to lose its status and become a colony (translated as "Slave Nation" in Bantu milieu), new political activities began taking place throughout the whole Nzadi basin (the Congo basin) within the new Mbôngi, "Church" institutions. A well documented, political, anti-Belgian imperialism underground or "Tèmbo" movement was born in Maniânga region. Nicolaï states that it was in 1906 that the missionaries (as state's agents) pointed out "Les premières manifestations d'hostilité (des Maniânga)"—The first manifestations of hostility in Maniânga.[6b]Under the leadership of Philippe Mbûmba, a catechist of Kinkènge (photo 1.),—after the Congo Free State became Belgian Congo—this underground, anti-colonial movement was intensified up to 1924, the year its leader was exiled in Belingo (Upper Zaire). The movement, implanted inside the "New Mbôngi"/the church, taught that colonization was against Congolese interests and that colonial agents were the first "Min'tantu" (enemies) of the people of Zaire, then the Congo: "L'administrateur de Luozi signale que dans le territoire, les Européens et particulièrement ceux de service territorial sont communément appelés, et ce depuis des nombreuses années: 'Mintantu,' ce qui signifie 'Ennemi' (Mithridate 1960:105)"* and elsewhere: "Mentalité des Maniânga: La population du territoire de Luozi se caractérise par un esprit d'indépendance plus accusé qu'ailleurs vis-à-vis des agents de

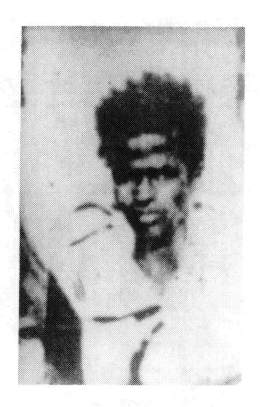

Photo 1: *Philippe Mbûmba (in his exile in Belingo, Upper Zaire), the most well known continuer-leader of the anti-Belgian underground political "Tèmbo" (movement) in Maniânga territory.*

Photo 2: Simon Kimbangu, the founder of the first massive, messianic-based political movement in Central Africa: the "Kintwâdi" (collectivism / socialism, togetherness).

The picture was taken in Lubumbashi (then Elizabethville) —where he died in exile—shortly before his "unspecified" death in 1951.

Photo 3: *From right to left Simon Kimbangu, Philippe Mbâmba, Andre Matswa, and Simon Mpâdi, all political leaders whose revolutionary action of each began under the umbrella of the "New Mbôngi." The meeting together and secretly of all these four Kôngo political leaders was very unique in circumstances in which they were labelled as "very subversive individuals" to the "Mission of Civilization," i.e. colonization and exploitation.*

l'Administration et par un défaut de considération à peine dissimulé"
(Op. cit. p. 102)*

In 1921 the catechist Simon Kimbangu (photo 2) began another
movement. It was a messianic-based political movement. This movement
was massive and more subversive politically. It was commonly known as
"Kintwâdi" and signifies in western languages "Communalism / Com-
munism, Union, Collectivism." Today the Kintwâdi of Kimbangu is
known under a new name, Kimbanguism, according to the name of its
leader.

It appears that in the 1950s, for the sake of its official status, the
organizers of the Kimbanguist church in its present structure preferred to
choose Kimbanguism as its official name rather than Kintwâdi—its first
and more controversial name—because its meaning in Kikôngo language
defined both as "Union/Collectivism" and "Socialism/Communism"
are concepts that the colonial government will never be pleased with.
Although Kintwâdi remains the official name used by the masses,
Kimbanguism is the name used by intellectuals and in bureaucracy to
define the deviation of Kimbanguism/Kintwâdi, (the political thought
of liberation) to the neo-Kimbanguism (the duplicate capitalist church in
Africa).

In the beginning the Kintwâdi had the main objective of political and
spiritual liberation of the oppressed in the Congo/Zaire in particular,
and of all Blacks in general (i.e. all of Africa).

Two decades after Kimbangu, a third catechist by the name Mpuyi, (of
the village Kingila, Sûndi-Lutete) and contrary to his predecessor
revolutionaries, began to attack the Christian doctrine itself. He
preached that the Christian religion was a "Yimbwa" (poison/opium) to
the growth of Black people. He went even further to, declare that
"Mbungulu," the hell, does not exist because our African ancestors, the
most religious people in the world, did not have a concept for it. His
doctrine was angrily assaulted by supporters of christianity. The song

---

*The administrator of Luozi territory points out that in the territory,
Europeans and especially those in territorial service are commonly
called, and this since many years: 'Mintantu,' which means
'Foes/enemies' and elsewhere "Mentality of Maniânga people: the
population of Luozi territory is characterized by a more independent
oriented mind than elsewhere vis-a-vis of agent of administration and by
a default of consideration almost impossible to dissimulate/hide." Cited
in Mithridate, R.B.: *Histoire de l'Apparition de Simon Kimbangu:
Documents Inedits 1921-'39;* Tome I, 1960, pp. 102-105; Ed. Notre
Kôngo Dièto, Kinshasa/Zaire.

below remains the only monument of those attacks:

Unionists (of the christianity)

Sirs!

Mpûyi read a book

There is no hell

In the sky (heaven)

Under modern neo-colonial oppression, in some instances, the church is still considered in many African countries not only as an institution of faith but also as a Mbôngi of refuge—a political umbrella—(photo 3) where people can discuss issues and problems related to their basic needs as well as their political problems (including plotting against a repressive regime). It is through this phenomenon (the movement of natives towards the church as a new form of Mbôngi) that one has to evaluate the success or the failure of christianism in Africa. In other words, the success of Western religion in the Third World in general and in Africa in particular is the result of oppression and torture. Torture through colonial and neo-colonial oppression is the key element to the success of Western religion in Africa. Perhaps this is one reason Western powers like to support anti-national interest dictators because the latter's action opens wide African doors to free exploitation of their nations' resources as well as their people. African nations are in trouble as long as they continue to sing words such as those from this couplet:

"Mbôngo za Nza yâyi

Ka zena ndându ko"

(translation)

Material goods of this world

Have no value at all.⁶ᶜ

In spite of its physical appearance, the Mbôngi is the strongest, most powerful, and the most authoritative institution known by the community Kânda cfr. "The Mbôngi is the center of the community" (proverb 1.18.) "The Mbôngi is the institution that teaches about the system of a community" (proverb 1.19), and "The Mbôngi is the heart of the community" (proverb 1.20.) The concept that this institution explains and transfers (explicitly and implicitly) the political organization of the community appears superior to its degrading physical appearance. It is traditionally the Mbôngi which transfers the power, the wisdom, authority and rights to the community and to its members. In the past it was the Mbôngi that was truly responsible for government's orders and regulations, not only within the community but throughout the country as well. All problems concerning organizational or practical issues in the community are first discussed in the Mbôngi before their approval or promulgation within the community. All community laws are made, approved and published from and by the institution of the Mbôngi. It is also the laws of Mbôngi (those laws which had a universal character) that were accepted as universal law at the level of "Mazându" (markets) in a given region or throughout a given African country.

Because of the value, authority, strength, and the power that the community holds in this institution, community youth are obliged to sit in the Mbôngi to learn the relations of the community institutions and its "constitution" politics, proverbs, experience, social alliances, wars, professions, techniques, wisdom, and "science." Wisdom and intelligence are taught and acquired through the Mbôngi according to this common saying "Sit in the Kiôto, where experience and proverbs on history and development are transferred" (proverb 5.9). Sitting in the Mbôngi is a social and political obligation of all for "The Mbôngi is the standardizer of the community life style" (proverb 1.14).

The most astonishing aspect of this institution to anyone sitting in the Mbôngi, or anytime a number of people gather there, is the concept of the *order* of what should be discussed. This practice gives us the idea of how the Mbôngi organizes its programs and its protocols, N'landa and N'sinda, within the community. During a single gathering in the Mbôngi, as many topics as possible are discussed (as "Lându," the schedule of the day). These topics range from diurnal activities of each community member present in the Mbôngi; community news and experience; news from neighborhood communities; community members living in cities; community policy and diplomacy related to "Mafula" (communities where sisters of the community are married) debates related to community youth life; questions concerning the land of the community; discussions related to the problems of life and death and also, comedies and jokes, animals and plants, activities and schedules of next day and the setting of dates for community programs to come. If such dates are fixed on certain days or weeks, Na Makolo (lit. the one who codes or ties knots) "ties" the knots (symbolic writings) to symbolize the time in days or weeks. At the end of everyday or of every week, according to agreements (Mabika/Ngwîzani) made or "tied up" by the community, Na Makolo unties or cuts one knot from the knotty rope of agreements (mabika, i.e. what was decreed or agreed upon) of the community programs.

It was a great responsibility of Na Makolo, the knots-maker, to recall for the community and the Mbôngi how much preparation they still have before the coming of the date and the event programmed by the Mbôngi, its authorities and its members. Na Makolo is also known as Na Mabika or Makôla, from "Bika" and "Kôla," respectively (to cite and to call/to pick up or to cut off) and both signify the one who not only recalls/announces but also cuts or cancels events and agreed dates.

To maintain the power of the unwritten constitution of the community, the Mbôngi holds the important responsibility of supervising the initiation (education) of the community youth, and to know the content of the initiatic program of each Kânga/Kôngo, the site of an initiatic school thoroughly. Because of such a responsibility, each Mbôngi among the Bântu once had its own "Lându" (course outline) for the youth of the Mbôngi in order to transfer the experience and proverb related to tradition, the documented history (figurines, knots, etc.), politics, diplomacy (Kinimalônde), and matters related to physical as well as to spiritual development, cfr. "Sit in the Kiôto where experience and proverbs on history and development are transferred" (proverb 2.9). Through this process, mastery of the language was also gained through the Mbôngi, because "The secrets of boko are not taught or discussed in a 'borrowed' language" (proverb 2.11). In modern Africa where this basic principle of all philosophies of education has no room, everything is *imposed* through borrowed languages.

This public and popular system of education in the Mbôngi holds great focus within the community because it aims to solve problems of the whole community. Such an education is also different from the one that is received from the "Buta" (family), cfr. "What is taught in the Kiôto builds the community substructure" (proverb 5.5) and "What goes within a household (its educational program) is different from what goes in the Kiôto" (proverb 5.7).

The Mbôngi, as the principal institution of the community, possesses its own leaders and their assistants (*"Mu bônga"*) to take care of community's and country's diverse responsibilities. These leaders are generally known by the general terms "Bambuta" or "Bakuluntu"—respectively, "Elders" and "Elders-at-the-head." They also are called "Mbuta-za-Mbôngi," elders or leaders of the Mbôngi or, sometimes, "Sîmbi bia Kânda," community jinni, community's dignitaries or community mandatories.

Some of the principal members of the government of this powerful tradional African instituion of Mbôngi are:

a/*Mfumu-mbôngi* (the chief of the Mbôngi)

The Mfumu-mbôngi, chief of the Mbôngi, is the symbol of the government of Mbongi itself. He can be considered as the president of the system of this African traditional political institution. The Mfumu-mbôngi or chief of the Mbôngi is the well known person of the institution and the most public figure of the Mbôngi government, but he is not the "person-pillar" of the Mbôngi. To know the principal pillars of the community and of the Mbôngi, one must go to "Ku Nènga" (the aside gatherings of the Mbôngi) where the Kânda commissions as well as those of Mbôngi meet. (Sometimes the pillars of the Mbôngi may be far from the community itself—workers, professors, etc. who only visit the community periodically). The Mfumu-mbôngi, chief of the Mbôngi, is always a solid individual in the local system. It is he who calls for community gatherings or for its commissions, "Mfûndu," in case of need.

He is the executive chief of the community constitutional orders, although his power is very limited: "Mfumu-mbôngi mpûngi a Kânda" (lit. The chief of Mbôngi is the community "horn") that blows to gather its members. As the horn of the community, he does not speak unless the community speaks through him. When the Mfumu-mbôngi, chief of the community, is absent, most of his responsibilities are supervised or carried out by his adjunct, "Lândi kia Mfumu-mbôngi" (the Mfumu-mbôni adjunct).

b / *Lândi kia Mfumu-mbôngi*

The "Mfumu-mbôngi-adjunct" is a community authority that comes after the Mfumu-mbôngi in the community Mbôngi to assist the latter or, in case of death or disease, to take over his duties and responsibilities. Very often this authority, the Mfumu-mbôngi-adjunct, is known outside of his social circle by the true name of the Mfumu-mbôngi preceded by the words "Lândi kia" (adjunct/vice of). For example to say "The adjunct of Mr. Muyembele," the social practice requires to one to say "Lândi kia Mwène Muyembele" or "Lândi kia Ta Muyembele;" to say "The adjunct of Mr. Makiôna," one must say "Lândi kia Mwè Makiôna." The person in this secondary position may also be called "Muyembele wanzôle/Muyembele II," the Second Muyembele; or "Makiôna ma II" for the Second Makiôna.

c / *Mfumu-dikânda* (the chief of the extended family)

The "Mfumu-dikânda" is a mandatory of his clan to the institution Mbôngi within an agglomeration made up of two or more lineages or extended families. He may also be both chief of his lineage and of Mbôngi as well.

The Mfumu-dikânda, chief of the extended family, and his adjunct are responsible for everything concerning their lineage or their extended family, the Kânda, and the position that this latter occupies within the union of Mbôngi and its constitution. The Mfumu-dikânda is a great community vociferator (Mfumu-dikânda m'bângadi); he has power at the head of his community and in front of its youth. He is the intermediary, N'kambakani, between the government of the Mbôngi and his own lineage, but also between his lineage in the physical or upper world and the ancestors' spiritualized community, the community of "Bakulu" (in the spiritual world, the lower world). The Bakulu are dead elders who, physically, spiritually, intellectually, and morally once reached a positive maturity of development in their process of Nkudulu (growth), the making of individual, but more important, also reached this level in their community or collective "Kikulu" (history/growth). As mediatory between these two sets of communities in two different worlds, the Mfumu-dikânda's main responsibility is a dangerous and mortal burden. It is to maintain the normal balance of the country (land)

and the community in such a way that the community "string," its structural foundation, is maintained and spread harmoniously everywhere. He operates through the above (the physical world) as well as in the below (the world of spiritualized ancestors, the spiritual world).

Thanks to his "four eyes," it is said that the Mfumu-dikânda has the power to see everything and make his burden bearable. Two eyes are to see and control his community in the upper world, the world of competition and of politics. The two others are to watch the world of "trickery," and to allow him to be in contact with the ancestors' world, the world of the accumulated human experience. Through this belief, every Mfumu-dikânda also becomes a Ndoki, the person that no one wants and no one hates because he is Nkasa (Erythropleum guineense) in the community. "No one drinks it; no one throws it away" hammers a Kôngo proverb.

By the order of the Mfumu-dikânda, the community can go to "talk" with its dead at their resting-place, the cemetary, in case of urgent need. In the past, again under his leadership, the community decided what "N'kisi" (field of knowledge/science) and techniques should be initiated in the community and by what "Ngânga," specialist. The Mfumu-kidânda also has the responsibility of supervising programs on questions of great interest to community: marriage, funerals, cooperation (Kitemo), gifts related to funeral feasts (Matanga), social or trading meetings, ceremonies, use of lands, fallow fields, etc. The Mfumu-dikânda is responsible for all his community members including their social behavior—in case of misbehavior of one of these members, the Mfumu-dikânda is the one who has to indemnify the offended side.

The following figure (fig. 2) gives an outline of the social structure of the lineage. A lineage or an extended family (Kânda) can be composed of a "Mwèlo-nzo" or many "Mièlo-nzo" (MN). At the head of each Mwèlo-nzo is the leadership/authority of "Nkâka," who is the family head. The Mwèlo-nzo can also have one "Môyo" or many "Miôyo" (M). The "Ngwa-nkazi," uncle, is the head of Môyo in matriarchal system. The "Môyo" can at its turn be composed of a "Buta" (B) or of many "Mabuta." The "Nkasi," old brother, is the head of the Buta. There are, in the Buta, the "Bâna" (b) called also "Bilesi bia Kânda," the community militants/agents. All members of a lineage belong to the same system be it matrilineage, patrilineage or bilineage.

d/ *Nzônzi* (the master of Kinzônzi)

There is another individual, very often a neutral outsider of the community who functions in the Mbôngi government. This individual plays a very important role in the shaping of the community and of the Mbôngi political philosophy. This is the "Nzônzi," a word not to be confused with "N'zônzi."

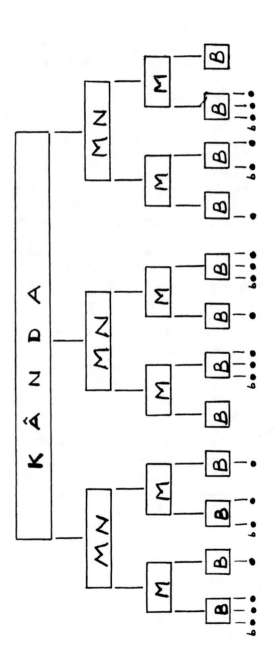

Fig. 2: Social structure of the "Kânda" or the community of biologically related members.

MN — the Mwêlo-nzo
M — the Môyo
B — the Buta ("family" in western sense)
b — the bilesi (community youth / militants) or bâna (children)

The term Nônzi, of the nominative class "N-Zi," is not the same thing as "N'zônzi" of the nominative class "N' (mu)—Mi." The latter means the one who speaks or talks ordinarily or a talkative person. But the former, Nzônzi, is a wise individual (a specialist) very skillful in matter and questions related to justice, decision-making, negotiation, law, punishment, counseling, and public-conflictual debates. He is eloquent, wise and knows many dialectical techniques used to discover the truth through the question-answer process. He is one of the most dignified figures in the Bantu system of the political philosophy in general and Kôngo in particular. He is the master of the *Kinzônzi* among the Bantu, the art of the truth finding. The Nzônzi is a specialist (photo 4). Kinzônzi is his domain of specalization.

Each Mbôngi has its Nzônzi, but can also have more than one. The Nzônzi of one Mbôngi can be member of one lineage or belong to another community (which is member of another Mbôngi). Because the Nzônzi of one community can be invited, "be borrowed," by one Mbôngi or another, he is, through his duties, obliged to study the customary and legal practices of the communities and Mbôngi not only of his region (jurisdiction) but of other regions as well. One Nzônzi can not be invited, "borrowed," in an area (jurisdiction) where he does not have knowledge about the social structure of local Mbôngi and their (unwritten) constitutions.

The Nzônzi is the speaker or the "mouth" of the Mbôngi and its constitution before all questions concerning custom, constitution and agreements of legal aspects in debating process, the "Nteolo a Kinzônzi." The Nzônzi of the Mbôngi and of the community is an individual who knows how to speak eloquently and also how to reply. He has mastered the art of "rolling" and of "unrolling"—coding and decoding—issues within the constitutional basis of the "Kisinsi" (system/custom) practiced in a given community/society. Through such mastery, he can pull out secret intentions of others and bring them to light through dialectic techniques. This is why the Nzônzi is also called "M'fûndi-a mâmbu," (the-one-who-digs-issues-like-a-pig,) but he is also the one who lightens and untightens issues; he is tough and flexible in the art of saying and of resisting, of taking and of remitting decisions concerning the community, the human society and its systems.

The principal function of the Nzônzi (the dialecticician-philosopher-politician-lawyer-legislator-judge-healer) in the community Mbôngi is to collect everything that is said and discussed in the regional Mbôngi where he practices his art of "Kinzônzi." Collected information allows the Nzônzi to interpret discussions in legal and constitutional language of the Mbôngi in question. In other words we say that it is the Nzônzi who tries to translate everything concerning the community and its Mbôngi

Photo 4: Official ceremony of "creating" a hearth: the marriage is a concern of communities and Mbôngi governments involved. Because children to be born from the hearth are members of the community, the ceremony which allows young people to create a "Buta" or family is not an affair of individuals. The creation of the hearth itself must be made publicly with the accord of the communitie involved before communities and Mbôngi governments concerned. The marriage here is not a "marriage on paper" [that one individual (lawyer) can easily tear up for his personal needs] it is a deep, community-based concern.

Standing in the picture are two Nzônzi engaged in "Nteolo a Kinzônzi" (debates) concerning the marriage. (Photo: J.M. Janzen, 1966.

language into legal terms in conformity with the constitution of the community.

Beside legal and constitutional interpretation functions, the Nzônzi has the responsibility of explaining the official policy of the community and its Mbôngi outside of the community zone (jurisdiction) in a manner which conforms to the law in order to make it understandable to all, those initiated as well as non-initiated. Because of his skill (specialization) in Kinzônzi, the art of Nzônzi or the knowledge about legislations and constitutions of Mbôngi and communities, the Nzônzi traditionally is considered among the Bantu (in general) and the Kôngo (in particular), as well as from afar, the most neutral of specialists. It is because of his neutrality and impartiality that the Nzônzi is sometimes invited or "borrowed" to plead for causes or to defend his clients in any area—as long as he has complete information about the (customary/unwritten) constitution of the community Mbôngi that invites him. A true Nzônzi has non-partial consideration because his role is to "hammer" the substructural philosophy of the Mbôngi which is "Lônda kânsi ka bâka ko" (To mend, but not to demolish). The greatest responsibility of the Nzônzi is to find out *"Kedika,"* the truth. Once that "Kedika" is found, the community Mbôngi decides accordingly.

Serious investigations directed by the Nzônzi could greatly help those who develop legal systems in modern Africa. Modern African states do not need either imported laws or constitutions essentially rooted on the basis of alien legal and ideological substructures. What Africa needs is to rethink its own traditional African legal and constitutional systems and put them in writing. Such laws and constitutions are already there in our "Fu-Kia-Nsi" or "Kisinsi" (customary laws and constitutions). No one can deny that. The very skillful people in the field, such as Nzônzi, can be of great help in the process of building modern African written laws and constitutions. These new laws and constitutions will, in their turn, form a new generation of Nzônzi for a new Africa.

e / *The N'swami*

In each Mbôngi there is a clandestine group of individuals who have diverse responsibilities for the security of the community and of its members. These individuals are called "N'swâmi" or authorities operating in secrecy. The term N'swâmi or Muswâmi (in the initiatic institution of Lèmba) indicates the assistant of the Ngânga-lèmba (a specialist in Lèmba). The principal role of these "under" authorities is to "spy," i.e. to collect information around the Mbôngi and its constitution. Among the N'swâmi, according to their professional particularities, one finds watchmen, investigators, and detectives, as well as spies. All these agents have the duty to counsel the community and leaders of Mbôngi. Hence, such agents are also called "Counselors."

The watchman known as N'kengi has a more integral role than simply focussing external concerns towards the community and its members. It is the N'kengi (watchman) who is responsible for community members' behavior among themselves and for the well-being of the community and of foreigners. The "N'langi" (from Langa, to inquire) is an individual whose greatest responsibility is to keep close watch on boundaries of the community lands and to report to the council of the Mbôngi any possible violation. The N'langi has to know precisely who does what and where on the lands as well as in community forests and waters, i.e. he knows almost everything going on in savannahs as well as in the forests of the community. The N'langi is also known technically as "Me-Zûmbu," the authority responsible for all questions related to community real estate.

Very often the "Me-Zûmbu" is also a skillful hunter or a great collector (tapster) of "Nsâmba," the "vegetal" milk from the palm-tree. Either one of these occupations requires him to have continual contact with all community properties (waters, lands and forests). His function is fundamentally based upon the constitutional principle expressed in the proverb "The community real estate cannot be alienated." Me-Zûmbu, the authority responsible for community land property, is a wise and intelligent individual. He knows the name of almost all animals, plants, birds, snakes, mushrooms, fruits, and fish found in community lands. He can distinguish them by their voices, cries, motions or by their footprints left on their pathway. He tells stories about them or imitates their voices and acts.

The N'suni, from "Suna" (to observe closely), is a very skillful individual who can follow or detect through footprints or "Lôbula" (directional information provided by the grass touched by a passer by), any person suspected of causing disorders within the community.

Beside the N'suni, there are also "N'neki," spiers. The work of the latter is external to the community and to the Mbôngi. The N'neki (spier) collects information from the outside of the Mbôngi and of its constitutional zone. Outside of their spying activities or "Kin'neki," the N'neki are petty traders and travelers. They like markets and gathering places. The Kin'neki is one of the means utilized by the Mbôngi to increase its knowledge of "Kinimalonde," which are outside community or regional relations and diplomacy.

When members of this group tell about news of their deeds, they are listened to with great attention by the community (primarily in the Mbôngi) because their reports may have a negative or positive impact upon the community life. After the N'neki's summing up, the responsibility of evaluating the accuracy of N'neki's report in accordance with the community constitution remains with the entire Mbôngi, not exclusively with the Mfumu-mbôngi, its leader.

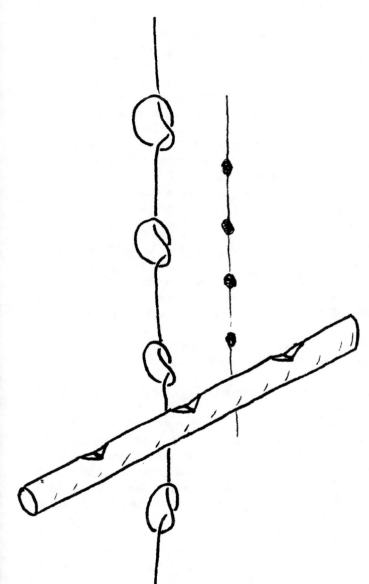

Fig. 3: Wood cuts and knotty ropes are parts of the Bântu iconographic writing system. The practice became complex in "Kinkete kia *Kânga* ye *Kutula* mâmbu" or the art of "Tying" and "Untying" social problems through Nkôndi, the nail-fetish.

f / Na-Makolo, "knotted information" archivist

In the past one could see an individual in the Mbôngi who was a member of the community named "Na Makolo" (or Makolo in short). This individual was very important to the community. He was the keeper of "knotted information," i.e. symbolically written information. This information-keeper individual could be called "secretary" or better, "archivist" in today's Mbôngi.

Any time the Mbôngi made a decision related to numbers of days, weeks, or months, set price or dates, the Mbôngi asked this individual, Na Makolo, to braid a cord and tie the number of knots which, in accordance with the decision made in Mbôngi, would represent the date set up for the next debate or meeting (fig. 3). If the Mbôngi had also concluded a contract of alliance with another Mbôngi, Ne Makolo was asked to represent that "Mandaka/Ngwîzani" (contract) by making knots on his braided rope (N'sing'a makolo) or simply in cutting marks (Makènko) on a piece of wood made for the purpose.

"Constitutionally" and in accordance to the way by which the Mbôngi system works, Na Makolo was obliged to know in detail the meaning symbolized by each knot which he ties or each cut that he makes. He was also required to decipher or decode the message symbolized by each knot on his knotty ropes. This practice was in common use among the Ngânga-nkôndi, the specialists in "problem hammering" among the Kôngo.[8]

If cuts and knots are made to represent recorded events, contracts or numbers related to the community well-being, knotty rope and pieces of wood bearing cuts representing circumstances are then given to Ne Masamuna, of "Samuna" (to speak out), the community griot (information and record recaller) or deposited in "Nzo-n'kisi," also called "Nzo-bakulu," the house of ancestors (i.e. house of history).[9] If they were given to Ne Mabika, of "Bika" (to announce)—the announcer of events according to time, the knots represented events' dates in days and weeks, anniversaries (bulungi), fining and the time at which payments should be made or problems rediscussed. Under these conditions, Mabika, the announcer, has the responsibility of untying or of cutting one knot at the end of every day or week according to the unity of the agreement until the last knot which represents the symbolic date of accord.

Both these individuals, Ne-Makôla and Ne-Mabika, watched over the constitutional power of the Mbôngi in all their activities. They had to "tie" (coding or writing symbolically) and "untie" (decoding or reading messages of knotty ropes) knots related to community and diplomatic matters in accordance to the order of the Mbôngi and its laws. To untie or cut one knot (decode a message) from teh contractual knotty rope, or add another knot was a crime which could lead its perpetrator to the market place, i.e. to the public court. This court alone had the right to make decisions on capital punishment which consisted of burying alive the guilty in the market place those who had violated these constitutional social responsibilities.

Many cases which prove knotted past-events of the community still exist in certain communities. In 1963, I left my teaching position in Kinshasa, the capital city of Zaire, and went to investigate the site in the area I had considered building Luyalungunu Lwa Kûmba-Nsi (An Institute for Higher African Studies). Upon arriving, I was surprised to find such knotted "documents" written in symbolic codes. for a certain period I stayed in Kûmbi, a village where I had my temporary provisory office (this village is the locality where I was born). Here, to my great astonishment, I found a very old lady by the real name Debola Zala (who is deceased) to be very sick. Knowing that she was approaching her death, she called Mr. Munzele, the chief of her lineage, in order to hand over him the historical documents of the lineage and the whole responsibility of taking care of them. These documents were knotty ropes and pieces of marked wood. What most struck my imagination was the explanation that Ma Zala gave from each rope and its knots as well as of the cuts on the wood. One would believe she was reading from a book. Knots "talked" about extended family's members *"sold as slaves"* (this expression should be understood as giving away as adoptees or as mortgage) and marks represented measures of animals given in the process. Some of the people mentioned in those knots were ransomed in the 1930's and are still alive today.

Although the use of knots, makolo, does not exist any more as a way of preserving information, it is not rare that in certain present Mbôngi one can see the practice of marking on wood, which serve as a demographic way of counting community members (its valid and unvalid population). The practice also comes in use when community goods, such as fruits, are shared.

On the basis of this tying and untying concept as an art, a related specialty has developed—that of Nkôndi, the "Kingânga-nkôndi." This speciality, in its coding and decoding or "hammering" process, uses a wrought object, the Nkôndi. The one who "ties," "unties" or "hammers" by Nkôndi is called "Ngânga-nkôndi." This is the specialist who ties and unties the "Mâmbu" or dealings inside as well as outside of the community.[10]

All agents forecited worked and are still working for the institution Mbôngi and for its constitution in order to develop it into a Mbôngi of hope and power, entrusted to a united group of "Zimbuta," elders/leaders. These elders (through their Kimbuta or seniority and experience) protect and take care of the institution of Mbôngi and its community constitution based upon the foundation of the local politico-economic system. Hence the native, i.e. the community member, is not exploited or deluded by illicit practices of internal and extenral anti-community forces.

To facilitate the functioning of elders in their responsibilities to Mbôngi and the community, every member of the community must be level-headed, and to understand everything concerning the constitution (custom) of the community Mbôngi: its material goods, its hierarchical order, its responisibilities, its rights, its politics, its organization and its authority, as well as its limitations. All youngsters of the community must be level-headed and sit in Mbôngi in order to learn and have one's eyes opened (Bulwa mèso) about community problems (as well as those of Mbôngi) cfr. "Sit on the Mbôngi's 'Kikulu' (lit. history) stool and then you will be able to tell Kikulu (history) of the community" (proverb 1.4). A variant of this proverb is "To have your eyes opened, sit in social institutions' assemblies" (proverb 1.16)—because it is the Mbôngi alone which possesses the "Siku" (measures of standardization) to regulate or to constitute the community and the country as well—cfr. "The Mbôngi is the standardizer of the community life style" (variant: "It is the Mbôngi that regularizes (stabilizes) the community life style" (proverb 1.14).

The Mbôngi institution is not only an educator or protector; it violently "vociferes" (punishes) when its members deviate from its "Siku," the norms and measures of standarized traditions and life within the community. As previously noted, an accused person in the past was brought to the market place, the public court, to be judged—and if found guilty, was buried alive. What is inconceivable, but true, is the fact that the Mbôngi administrative policy did not (as it does not today) have any concept of prison. The word "prison" itself does not exist in Bântu languages, because the community believes that jailing does not help solve problems—it only destroys and kills the human inner-being. Therapeutic ceremonies, in most cases, were more important rather than jailing or killing.[11]

The institution Mbôngi of the Bântu is not only a physical construction squatting in the middle of a village, it is an institution with very profound roots within the Bântu system of thought. The Mbôngi, as well as its authority, is present everywhere to the Bantu; even when they are not near its physical presence. Everywhere the Bântu system of organization exists, *there is also the call of Mbôngi*, i.e. a call for community cooperation, for better or for worse; "The call of Boko belongs to all of us" (proverb 2.1). This call once gathered and wants to continue gathering communities in order to regulate (constitute) all which is proper to the "Kisinsi"—and this call is to all African communities and their systems in order to organize, protect, educate and insure development upon Mbôngi's principles. This call must be heard (photo 5).

Photo 5: *"Mbila ku Mbôngi," the "Call of Mbôngi." The community of Sûndi-Buyala (Kivûnda/Luozi) holds a Fôngo before its Mbôngi. The standing man in the circle is the Nzônzi-a-Mfûndu addressing the Fôngo on Mfûndu (commission) report. Sitting on the table (far right near the Mbôngi shelter) is the author with his assistant.*

    Traditionally all human problems (issues) are an object of public hearing or debate in the Mbôngi, the community-parliament (Photo: J. M. Janzen, 1966).

Mbôngi

The author of *Man in Africa,* Turnbull, said "The power of tradition is the power to keep Africa alive."[12] He was not mistaken. Elsewhere he states "In understanding the past we can better understand the present."[13] An African government which is not founded upon the basis of its own local system or systems is a government founded upon a Mbongi of "N'kuyu," the bad and stunted ancestors. This is a Mbôngi which does not have any "spur," or inspiration. Such a government is unable to develop the country or its communities. Soon or later one will see that such a government was actually carcinogenic to the nation and to its people as well.

CHAPTER III
POLITICAL ORGANIZATION OF MBONGI

In the Bântu-Kôngo system, the concept of social and political community in the midst of Mbôngi would be inconceivable without the freedom and right of self-criticism (Ntungasani) warranted by this institution. An old proverb states "A Mbôngi where self-criticism is not tolerated is strange and inconceivable" (proverb 1.8). By this principle, the Mûntu individual learns through the constitutional organization of Mbôngi that there is no place for "Kimonkwâmi," the egotistic "I" of monopolism, be it expressive, economic or politic. What community members say or transfer becomes a portion of the cultural heritage commonly built upon by all members of our community (dead or alive). This is the common heritage to which we refer when we say "Bambuta bata ngana" (Our ancestors have said). This is a collective expression of physical as well as spiritual unity to which each of us will become part after death.

Traditionally the Mbôngi is the principal organizing institution of community politics. Its power regulates the internal as well as external social life of the Bântu. A Kôngo proverb states "The Mbôngi takes all problems of the community," and a variant reads, "It is the Mbôngi that discusses social conflicts in the community" (proverb 1.1).

Throughout the whole organization of the Mbôngi as well as its constitution, lies what is called 'Ntungasani," self-criticism. Freedom of speech and of expression are the first principles in debate or conversations in the Mbôngi. Absolutely everyone, in the midst of this institution has the right of speech with absolute respect. Old or young, male and female all have the right of the "word" in the Mbôngi. It is of legal power (in the Kôngo Mbôngi) not only to sit in but to express one's opinion as well while sitting in the community Mbôngi.

It is clear that because of her diverse daily responsibilities (not only familial, but also domestic/sparing as well as economic), the political activity of females in the Mbôngi, given limited time, are and were slight. The woman's major participation as a political member of the Mbôngi government remains that of counselor, keeper of valuable documents (such as "Makolo," knotty ropes), and witness in many cases (mostly those related to land, forest, and diplomacy of the community). This is for the simple reason that 1). Women are most in contact with the community lands? 2) They are respected as the best farmers according to the African agricultural practices;[14] and 3) For economic reasons and for their skill in management of family affairs.

Without the participation of the woman, feasts would be impossible in the African world, for she is not only the cook but the one who provides the most food for the community. By her displacement to her husband's community from her mother community due to marriage, the Bântu woman is well placed to deal with many "diplomatic" issues between communities or regions—especially between her permanent or maternal community and her provisory or marital community.

The policy of Mbôngi and its community organization is seen from afar as powerful, strong, and more stable than that of many African modern governments which have been installed with the help of machine-guns provided by Moscow and Washington. The Mbôngi political structure is strong and self-sufficient because it is based on African reality, the local system of the thought, and on the other hand, stems from a solid *common aspiration* served by each community member: to keep the community united on the motto basis of "Ntungasani ye Ntwalasani" (Self-criticism and Co-leadership), which is, in reality, profoundly solid and the foundation of community power which keeps it above corruption.

For a community united through the physical, political or social Mbôngi, corruption or the corruptibility of a community is a cancer which can attack and completely destroy any community through all means and at all levels, until it becomes the total destruction of the community and the country as well. Corruptibility is shameful within a community. It intimidates, and there is neither success nor possible development through intimidation because it destroys completely.

Well aware of the danger and miseries that can be introduced to a community through this political cancer (which attacks through corruption and illicit payments), the traditional Mbôngi prefers to carry out the leading of the country and its communities by ways of "Mfûndu," or commissions/ cabinet-groups instead of "Kidingizi" or ministeries. It should be said that the Bantu people, who are aware of their traditional systems, know that it is easier to corrupt or to exploit ministerial policy led by one individual than a policy led by "Mfûndu," commissions, or cabinet-groups. There is a saying "The commissions of Mbôngi which reveal social problems and their causes are incorruptible" (proverb 1.15). The individual member of a community, no matter who he may be, can easily be corrupted. But it is not easy to corrupt the whole "Mfûndu" (i.e. all its members) without causing "Mawele-wele" (a hubbub).

Before discussing the existing difference between the concept of "Mfûndu" and that of "Kidingizi" among the Bântu (according to their social and political organization of the Mbôngi—traditionally the most important political institution that remains alive in today's Africa), we must first examine the latter, the Kidingizi political system.

A/ *The politics of Kidingizi*

The "Kidingizi" political system is a system in which governments prefer dividing their responsibilities into "Nkutu"—literally, "sacks of goods/wealth" or portfolios. Each Nkutu or "Ngûmbu" (House/cabinet) must have an individual head responsible for the Nkutu. This individual is known as "dingizi" or "Sièlo," minister/servant. His institution and authority constitute the "Kidingizi/Kisièlo," his "ministry."

In this political system, the Dingizi has the responsibility to organize, lead, and look after the responsibilities of his Kidingizi (ministry). He has the right to choose employees and counselors who must work in his cabinet in order that the "Nkutu"[15] of his institution would not be oppressed by other Nkutu. He is also responsible for all political and diplomatic decisions of his "Ngûmbu," cabinet. In his position as Dingizi, he also had the right (in accordance to the national constitution) of receiving citizens and foreigners in or outside of his cabinet, publicly or in private, to discuss questions concerning the country which are linked to his "Ngûmbu" (competence.) In all these dealings the Dingizi acts in terms of the monopolistic "I", i.e. he acts *alone.*

Do consider the relationship of the underlined word, alone, to the policy of concern to developing countries. People in these countries are "hungry" for everything: hungry for power, hungry for prestige, hungry for goods, hungry for a little of this and for that. The political system of the Bântu people, through Mbôngi institutions (with their traditional or oral constitutions), did not opt for the policy of Kidingizi political system because Bântu people, in their political experience, know that it is very easy for community and national authorities (primarily at the ministerial level/Kâmba kia Kidinigizi) as individuals, acting *alone*, to become corrupted. And this is because of the "cloth" of "Kimonokwâmi" cited above—the individualistic or monopolistic leadership which leads towards social, political, economic, and systematic corruptibility among leaders—the disease of which all of Africa is suffering from today.

Such a policy based upon the egoistic "I" does not fit into modern Africa because it does not have roots in African traditional political organization. Secondly, such a policy facilitates the exploitation of natives who have already been made very poor and wretched by colonial and neo-colonial exploitation. Finally, this policy reinforces the bureaucracy and urbanization of Africa, two large agents of dehumanization and primary sources of corruption. Because of this policy, which consigns the responsibilities of a ministerial cabinet to one single individual in a Third World country (who is very often busy with his "Makângu"/ Mistresses, whereby he keeps the public from discovering his uncompetency) many African countries have today, lost not only their security, but even the once common political concept of sharing power and energy collectively in their key institutions.

Many other "modern" anti-social ailments have also invaded the whole continent. Elders as well as youngsters have learned how to deceive, rob, kill, and cross one's hands. Everyone now seems to want to leave their job to become ministers or presidents in order to have, Africans say, "the official" right of lying, torturing, and robbing the nation without being incriminated before community law or the government. With the present "Kimonokwâmi"/"Kimonomosi" (the political monopolism) to whom they attribute themselves, new African leaders have the right to act as they choose and sell national material goods and documents. They believe that after them the end of the world will come. What a crime that world powers support such inhuman regimes! Unfortunately, these are the same regimes that Moscow and Washington would certify as being the most progressive as far as "human rights" are concerned.

Authorities at the cabinet level in all governments working under this so called "Kidingizi" political system are also corruptible in their ministerial activities. This policy is disliked among the Bantu because time and experience have taught them that authorities operating under such a system tend toward imposing a dictatorship.

B/ *The politics of Dictatorship.*

Dictatorship is a political and administrative practice which leads political authorities of monopolistic systems to impose their orders, good or bad, upon their so called "underlings." It is very rare that these authorities listen to what comes from the "bottom" of the political mountain, avoiding though to draw one's inspiration from "Luvèmba" and "Kala" which are closer to the historico-cultural inspiration of the past, the "Musoni," which is illustrated in fig. 4. Under these conditions, the "Tukula" (modern African leadership) is inhibiting because it rebels against African political systems and against the concepts of economy experienced by these systems throughout the continent.

"A dictatorship is not barren" says the Kôngo wisdom. It causes another source of ailment—violence—through its monopolistic policy.

Authorities which come to power by force use violence to reinforce their regimes. Under the cloak of violence, the government uses inhumane procedures to silence the people's voice. Such means include tortures;the imprisonment of those who attempt to criticize government behavior; the erection of road barriers throughout the country; the secret elimination of people; the assassination of those willing to think for their communities as well as for their country; the intimidation of people to force them to accept and/or to provide false testimonies; the development of the army—the number one enemy of the people; the establishment of educational programs which lack any substance except that of empty propaganda.

After completely oppressing the people and the entire country in such a way that everything is controlled by the will of the "regime," authorities then look forward to the next political step: becoming publically visible. They announce their "official titles" to all those without such titles. They wish to build empires (Bimfumu-mayâla) in order to become "Mfumu-mayâla," or chief-of-chiefs—the authority-of-authorities, the emperor.

C/ The Politics of the "Kimfumu-mayâla."[16]

Dictatorship and violence produce envy in every authority involved—an envy to govern for life with the attempt of even becoming willing to suppress the idea of being mortal. Such leaders want to become a "God," the principle of life and initiator of change. Once such envy (power) becomes mature, it leads authorities of this form to change their titles and assert themselves a grandeur that is nothing but a void and a degradation.

The "Kimfumu-mayâla" is a chiefdom under the power and authority of "Mfumu-mayâla," the authority-of-authorities, i.e. the agent of imperialism by excellency. In such a state, there is no expression and no voice stemming from the community and from its inhabitants. A sole voice is heard—that of "Mfumu-mayâla," the emperor himself and his "Mayâla," the opportunists (allies) of the regime.

"Kimayâla," the authority of "Mfumu-mayâla," can also be defined as imperialism. Wherever this tendency exists, one sees widows and orphans in high numbers, and famine, diseases and death at a level that no human language can describe. Ceremonial programs are numerous, not only to prevent people from thinking rationally but, also, as a "brainwashing" technique.

*

*   *

In the region I am originally from (Luôzi territory, in Lower-Zaire), there was a chief of emperor-like tendencies whose real name was Kinânga—also known as Mfumu Kinânga (Chief Kinânga). I remember this chief from my childhood (when he was already in his latter seventies) but did not "taste" his authority because I was from a different chieftancy. Elders who knew the authority of this chief still shake their heads: "He was," they always say, "an authority -of- authorities." Our informants (in the chieftancy of Kiniangi where the above mentioned was chief) state that anytime this chief was on official tour, the whole region became panic stricken—because he could take by force whatever pleased his imperialistic tendencies: food, animals or women (married or not). He jailed husbands and fiancees of snatched ladies. When this same chief wanted to eat or to speak, he sat with his feet on the back of the prisoners of the bloody Belgian colonial system he served. Inhabitants of this chieftancy finally rebelled, and his authority was destroyed forever.

*   *

*

D/ *Reactions to the Politics of Kimayâla and Mfumu-mayâla.*

It is always a fact that through menacing their people and countries, authoritarian regimes prepare the ground-work among the masses for the following reactions:

1) Murmurs and critiques:

"Murmurs" and critiques are the first symptoms manifest by a people as reaction of disapproval towards unliked policies. These symptoms, in the case of Black Africa, have produced songs as well as secret code-names attributed to the authorities involved or disliked. These names and songs which serve to criticize unwanted leaders or countries with oppressive regime are both a call and a message transferred secretly and symbolically to community members in order to express rising dissatisfaction throughout the country. (Interesting studies could be made on the development of such songs and names as reactions to today's African regimes.)

Critiques expressed through such songs are a secret call to "Ku Nènga," (a site-spot, away from disrupting activities, where serious social problems and issues are discussed), inviting people to take a stand or action that would not only save communities, but the entire country and its acceptable systems. In "Ku Nènge" the truth, absolutely all the truth, must be revealed in order to find means and ways necessary to protect the community, its members and its system as well. When governmental abuses and corrupt political and administrative practices are well known, antagonism arises between national authorities and the masses which eventually lays the ground-work for the people to rebel overtly (against the despotism of the system.)

It is almost impossible to talk about African people today, or to try to predict what they may do tomorrow without consideration of what is being conveyed, concerning African modern regimes and their supporters, through songs and symbolic names addressed to their leaders. "Power is pitiless. Yet those who abuse it eventually walk down the gangplank."[16b] The rise of dictatorship today, in Africa, will be impossible without the support of the African intellectual opportunistic class and the assistance from business sector (banks, corporations, agencies) operating in the continent. And there is a lot to compare with Hitler's rise: It was largely middleclass apathy and support of big business...that helped the Nazis to power, states Anna Tomforde.[16c]

2) The "Lukolomono":

People of all nations and all societies around the world learn how to "Kolama" (to rebel). To rebel is to disobey a legal or a self-imposed government when needs and rights of people are trampled upon and government policy deviates from social values and from communities' constitutional rights (in case of Africa, the rights of the Mbôngi, which constitute the footing of the concept of the "state" itself). When this desire to rebel, Kolama, is present throughout the country, riots explode like volcanoes. As the Kôngo say: "Lukolomono ka sita ko," the rebellion is not barren.

Lukolomono politically is nothing other than the reaction of an oppressed people (for the sake of political as well as economic solutions) to a situation of misery created by insane policies. The "Lukolomono" (rebellion) is always fostered by the very regime against which it fights. In the case of Africa this rebellion has two big targets: dictatorship (Kimayâla) itself and the big business's exploitation (Kinwuki) that fosters and supports the former. For all that, one must understand that "N'kângu kanangumuka N'kele mikitukidi bipôpo" (When people rebel bullets become snow balls), states a Kôngo proverb. Firearms always fail before the uprising of just cause.

3) Revolution:

When the aforementioned symptoms and conditions are united, they often lead to mass revolution. The hope of a positive change in the people's situation (into which they were plunged by systems which often do not have roots in their main beliefs and concepts) lead many modern people to a revolutionary situation.

Many recent African revolutions have led to the arrest of authorities and the repossession of all goods robbed from the people. Such revolutions have also attacked alien governments who have supported the institutions of national despotism—seizing or nationalizing such governments' properties. "Knots" and "notches" of diplomatic relations are then *unknotted* and literally set fire—i.e. diplomatic relations are deferred or simply terminated. Mbôngi and their systems are restored and a new policy takes up the responsibility it has to protect the country or communities' constitution—which is founded upon the Mbôngi, the public common-council-house. Following such a pattern can be the only way for a dehumanized nation to rediscover its "Kisinsi," the traditional system, in order to build a local system renewed technically, politically, and scientifically.

Political and cultural revolutions are not recent in Africa, and yet they have not been imported through "nuclear technology." The African tradition tells a lot about revolutions in the past. All revolutions are not identical, but four facts are true for all revolutions, be they well orchestrated or improvised:

1. Revolutions take place anywhere there is dictatorship based on antinational interest, and exploitation of man by man.
2. Revolutions always lead towards a change, be it positive or negative.
3. A successful revolution is a shared action.
4. Each revolution has a "Sîmbi," a charismatic figure, as its leader.

Leading a revolution is an art and many revolutionary pretender-leaders fail before this art. Revolution itself is a *very sweet word* and thus it is easier to make a worse revolution than a good revolution

Irregardless of the type of government they have known in the past or present, the Bântu people live a federalistic life politically and economically (Zîngu kia Ndatasani/Nsalasani) *within and between* their ethnic regions. Their federation (Kindatasani) can be understood today from a rural community level, and at the policy level of the Mbôngi.

In my personal experience as a member in the "Kibântu" (the Bântu system of thought, their philosophy), and as a native belonging to a sub-Bântu cultural group, the Kôngo, I have not known a single community which has or has had a despotic policy. though there is no single community Bântu which is ready to abandon its policy of "Mfûndu (of Mbôngi), the Mfûndu policy can substitute for "Kimfumu-mayâla"—the source of disorder and corruption which is dehumanizing the all of Black Africa today. Modern African regimes and their political and economic concepts constitute a mortal poison for the development of free continental Africa.

E/ *The Politics of "Mfûndu."*

The "Mfûndu" is the cornerstone of the politics within societies belonging to the Bântu system of thought and decision making process. Among the Bântu-Kôngo, the terminologies "Kinzônzi" and "Mfûndu" are dialectically inseparable. They resemble one another as the bracelet does to the arm, or the rope to the waist.[17] Where there is "Kinzônzi" (politico-dialectic debates/politics), there are "Mfundu" (dialectical commissions/sessions of debates). And where there are Mfûndu, there is Kinzônzi. It is the Mfûndu and the Kinzônzi—the politico-dialectic art, not only of finding the truth but of leading public affairs as well—that together make the good government of Mbôngi for the community and for its members.

The Mfûndu policy has a permanent "seat," the institution Mbôngi. For the Bântu, the government is entirely in the care of the institution called Mbôngi. It is from this institution, which shares its power in branches of authority (in order to facilitate and distribute the weight of its responsibilities) that the Mfûndu policy draws its resources. The order which the Mbôngi serves for Mfûndu is an order that expresses the will not solely of Mfumu-mbôngi, the president of the Mbôngi, but of all community-members of the Mbôngi. Daily community activities are discussed by the entire Mbôngi and its "Zimbuta" (dignitaries), and social problems of the community and of the country (region) are regularized there as well. The Zimbuta lead the community policy according to the will expressed by the Mbôngi social system and by its unwritten constitution. One must point out here that the Mbôngi pays great attention to opinions expressed by its youth (future community leaders) during the gathering of the Mfûndu sessions in "Ku Nènga" (the site-spot for serious dialectical debates).

Special questions and problems of the community do not follow general procedures. In other words, those problems are not discussed during the "Bûndu/Fôngo" (the assembly of Mbôngi). They are directed to special "Mfûndu" (commissions) and are "dug" (Fûndwa/Sâtwa) by wise individuals, i.e. elders and specialists who are from the community, or "borrowed" from the neighboring communities. When one of these Mfûndu is taking place, people who are not members of the Mfûndu (commissions) can still sit in as auditors or observers.

After the Mfûndu debates, it lies with the speaker of the Mfûndu known as "Mpovi-a-mfûndud" or "Nzônzi-a-mfûndu" to give his "Lukofi" (a gesture which consists of clapping hands while on one's knees) when the assembly is reconvened. The gesture itself is an esoteric symbol of reverence used for "demande d'audience," or the right to speak. Immediately after the acceptance of "Lukofi" by the assembly (Fôngo/Bûndu), the speaker of Mfûndu will start the presentation of his report—"seasoned" with mottoes, songs and proverbs.

The "Nzônzi-a-mfûndu" or "Mpovi-a-mfûndu," the speaker of the Mfûndu, is always nominated after Mfûndu debates (on the Mfûndu spot) by the members of that particular Mfûndu, who base their choice upon the individual's competency and knowledge about the issue debated. After he has been pointed out or nominated by his colleagues (members of the Mfûndu), the Mpovi-a-mfûndu will take the full responsibility (Yeko/mbebe) for presenting the Mfûndu report in the Mbôngi, where the "Fôngo" (the assembly of the community) and many other wise community people and specialists wait for what the Mfûndu has "dug out" (Sengumuna/Fundumuna) from the issue presented to them. As with many other important aspects of the Bântu political philosophy, this aspect of "Bântu dialectics" within political and judiciary procedures has not yet been fully explored by scholars and / or politicians.

The following figure (fig. 4), the first illustration of its sort ever printed, gives details of the esoteric nature of the organizational structure of the Bântu political and judiciary system in its relation with Mfûndu. The illustration reflects the cosmological concept which generates the all of the Bântu system of thought as it is practiced among the Kôngo people. The illustration also reveals the foundation and the organization of the Mbôngi government. This institution still remains hidden and unknown to the political world of modern Africa. Yet it is this Bântu system and its world view which made possible the rise of powerful empires and kingdoms in an "illiterate" Africa before colonization: A Mbôngi and a "government" in each community (fig. 5), which served *community* interests before instructing a national standing army. Most Bântu states did not have "standing armies" because of their humanistic concepts and beliefs which put primacy on *man, his life* and *his community*.

According to the Bântu concepts, the Mbôngi is a gathering together of the dead (their radiated spiritual presence) and the living community-members to regulate and balance the community's and country's problems. Community "Mfûndu" (commissions) take place to examine social problems and counsel relatives about decisions to be taken for the community and for its members. This is why "Zimbuta"/wisemen sit at the Mfundu. These people are also called "Bankwa-mvu mu mayîndu," people whose mind is "gray" (mature) in spite of 'Luvèmba,'[17b] (the negative element accumulated in them by the fact of age.)

For its part the community holds the principal role of approving or disapproving the decisions of the Mbôngi; to allow them to be executed by its members in order to form a "Kala,"[18] burning coal, flaming inside the Mbôngi at its fireplace which turns into "Kala-zima,"[19] literally charcoal, i.e. the catalyzer of the power that extinguishes (catalyzes) conflicts and antagonisms within the system of the community and country).

The Mbôngi itself is the principal institution of decision making, of community order, and of direction towards "Tukula"—the red-symbol of biological life and of growth, not only physical and spiritual, but political, economic and technological as well. This is also the meaning of "Kula" (to grow) in its deepest and most thought-provoking sense.

The ancestral spirit with its radiations inside the Mbôngi is a source of inspiration to community members in their activities, their projects, and their dreams for better life. It is thought that this ancestral radiated presence in Mbôngi prints (sona) in the minds of youngsters (Bilesi) that which builds and develops a community because this radiated spirit is the "Musoni" (yellow), the symbol of the human experience accumulated at "Ku Mpèmba" (the universal world of inspiration) by the historical and

46

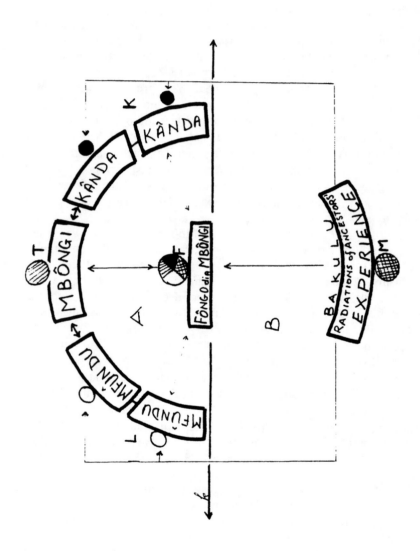

Fig. 4: The Kôngo cosmologically-based structure of the traditional Community Mbôngi Government; a structure that survived the colonial domination.

A—the physical or upper world, a political world.

B—the ancestro-spiritual world, an a-politic world but whose "radiations" are the community's best source of reference.

M—represents "Musoni," the symbol of the world of radiations and accumulated experience of the past.

K—represents "Kala," the symbol of vitality, growth, and of survival under a "burning" sun/world.

T—represents "Tukula," the symbol of maturity, power, and awareness.

L—represents "Luvèmba," the symbol of wisdom and maturity of mind in "dying bodies" (elders in Mfûndu).

k—represents "Kalûnga," the mystic wall separating the physical (upper) and spiritual (lower) world.

O —represents community Institutions and Commissions of study and consultations.

◉ —represents institutions of decisions, execution, and direction (leadership)

● —represents institutions of approval, application, and control (i kala ye kalazima).

⊗ —represents institutions of inspiration, dreams, and reference for new insight.

⊗ —represents "Fôngo," the institution of public debates, and approval; but also the community constitutional body.

cultural past of the living community.

The "Fôngo," or the community assembly is the institution which assembles or brings together all the real and symbolic forces which react reciprocally in politics and in organization of the Mbôngi: those of Kala (K), Tukula (T) and of Luvêmba (L) in the upper or physical, visible and political world, as well as those of Musoni (M) in the lower or ancestro-spiritual, invisible and apolitical world (fig. 4).

Because these forces do unite to constitute and "hammer out" community and Mbôngi "constitutional" decisions, the "Fôngo" of Mbôngi, (F) where such forces are gathered, became the fundamental "N'kisi" (medicine) for all *politics* of the society, its government and its culture. It is in the Fongo of Mbôngi that political debates, approbations, or disapprobations take place because it is this assembled Fôngo that also holds the *constitutional power* within the community. Of all decisions made at Mbôngi, its authorities never lack reference to what was already decided or known by the ancestors in politics of organiza-tion—for as it is said, "Bakulu, the great ancestors, in all Bântu societies, are the social sources of reference and spur."[19b] Hence, the Fôngo often relies on the various expressions: "Our ancestors have said that; the experience has proved that; it has been said in the past by our ancestors that..." (Bakulu bata ngana vo...). These expressions

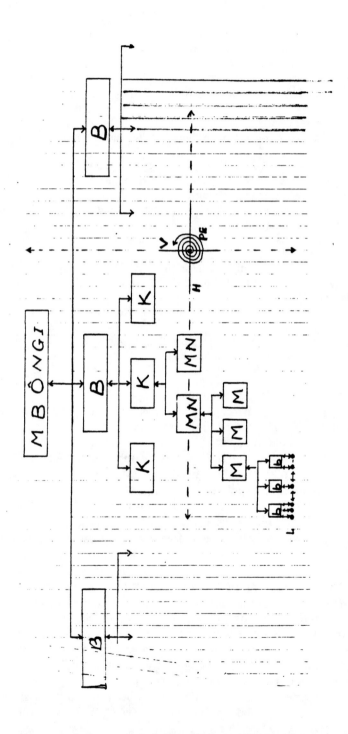

Fig. 5: The physical, Kôngo traditional structure of the Mbôngi government: Each "Sikudusu" (institution) is a collectively run organ; even the Mûntu (individual) himself, must perpetually be "shaped." He though remains a "Lesi" or a perpetual learner in his environment.

B   —the Belo (ward of a village)

K   —the Kânda or the community of biologically related members.

MN—the Mwèlo-nzo

M —the Môyo

b   —the buta (family in western sense)

L   —the Lesi (community youth/militants)

PEHVS—political Power and Economy are Horizontally as well as Vertically Shared through all community social layers.

introduce, verify, justify or present a statement, a finding, a decision, etc. before the gathering community members.

CHAPTER IV
MFUNDU AND ITS DIVISIONS

We must again first realize that, for the Bântu, the institution of Mbôngi is the center of community thought—the popular thinktank of the traditional governmental political systems in all collective Bântu societies. It is the location of Mbôngi which is the legal and permanent seat of the Fôngo (assembly of the community). The Fôngo of Mbôngi is above all community Mfûndu; it has a "constitutional" power to reject a decision made by Mfûndu (commissions conducted by the same wisemen, elders, who conduct the assembly of Mbôngi).

With all politics relating to the government of Mbôngi and its relationship with the community, there lies a basic analogy: the assembly of Mbôngi and the Mfûndu are alike as oil and salt are on the hands of the community—none of them can be thrown away. The Fôngo never bypasses collective authority and the Mfûndu never disobeys the constitutional order of collectivity throughout the Mbôngi's Fôngo. As community institutions, each has mutual obligations to the community and the country in order to defend and insure their security and their material, human and spiritual prosperity.

Mfûndu commissions are branches or divisions in the administrative organization of the Bântu political system (especially among the Kôngo). They consist of groups of people chosen to deal with types of problems linked to their competencies or past political or administrative experience in affairs of the community. It is hard for outsiders of such a system to fully understand how the Mfûndu of a community function within the Mbôngi political system, because a few or many individuals can sit in their bosom. The Mfûndu, however, holds the executive responsibilities before the community constitution of which the *Mbôngi is the executive power*. Only 3 to 5 individuals can be responsible for and in a Mfûndu commission. These individuals are known as "Mfumu-za-mfûndu," leaders of Mfûndu.[20] Those chosen responsible to conduct the

Mfûndu have the responsibility to report before the gathering of the community *on all* decisions taken by the Mfûndu of whom they are authorities and masters. These individuals, members of Mfûndu, are "ministers without portfolio" (Madingizi/Sièlo kôndwa Nkutu). Their role in the Mfûndu can be seen as constituting a Ngûnbu/Nènga, a cabinet or a "ministerium," led not by a sole minister in the sense of the egotistic "I" but by a commission of collaborating members of 3-5 people (the Mfûndu) according to their speciality and to their "Kinzônzi" competency. They are "co-ministers" of the Mfûndu with equal status before the government of the Mbôngi, the constitution, and before their constituency as well. No decision can be taken, approved, or "hammered" (signed) at the institutional level of Mfûndu if one of its members is absent in the "Ngûmbu/Ku Nènga," the "cabinet" of Mfûndu.

Beside the leaders-of-Mfûndu (Mfumu-za-Mfûndu) there sits another group of individuals of great influence for the politics of Mfûndu—that is the group of witnesses-of-Mfûndu and counselors. The role of this group in Mfûndu is constitutionally defined by the "Mfumu-za-Mbôngi," leaders of Mbôngi institution.

When the Mfûndu presents its report at the Fôngo of Mbôngi, all its principal members and their witnesses must be also present in order to confirm their unanimity on the decisions described within the verbal report of the "Mpovi-a-Mfûndu"[21]—the speaker of Mfûndu. This speaker addresses the assembly and the "Mfumu-mbôngi," the chief of Mbôngi who, in reality, is the president (N'kukuniûngu) of this type of government and leader of community policy. the Mfûndu report addresses itself, however, to the whole community.

A sole member of Mfûndu cannot gather the Mfûndu at the "Bèndo kia Mfûndu"[22] or spot/site of Mfûndu to receive visitors or discuss any problem by that name when other members are absent. To violate this practice is to commit a crime before the community and before the constitutional organization. To "go aside" (Kwènda ku Nènga/ku Mfûndu) is an art that consists not only of consulting the ancestors (i.e. the "rolls of accumulated experience within the spiritual "hole" or cultural bank of the past),[23] but also of initiating the youth in this art of "going aside" (Ngyendolo ku Mfûndu/ku Nènga) to dig out serious issues and problems relating to the community and its neighborhood. In other words, this is a primary way of preparing forces in the Art of Decision Making for the new society to come which must "maintain braced or stretched the community rope/string" (Nîngisa n'singa dikânda) and its balance (Kinenga kiândi) in good harmony between "Ku nseke ye ku mâmba"—the physical (the upper) and the spiritual (the lower) worlds.

Through procedures of reporting to the people's Mbôngi Assembly, members of a Mfûndu can succeed themselve in turn as speakers of their Mfûndu. The speaker of the Mfûndu must use oral presentation—interrupting his speech with mottos, proverbs and songs which give the dynamism of the "Kinzônzi" itself—the art of dialectically presenting political or judiciary reports. With the introduction of modern writing skills, the concept of a willingness to report by writing has slowly taken root inside the Mbôngi system which not only invades the "oralism" of the politics of the Mbôngi system, but also destroys the "Kinzônzi" art itself, the most important and exciting philosophical aspect of the Bântu dialectics with their political and judiciary process of "popular hearings."

We defined the term "Mfûndu" as a group of authorities of the political system of the Mbôngi. These authorities are chosen according to their experience/competence and their speciality in a domain, due to their ideas and intentions for the community and country (region), as well as their abilities to make sound decisions about problems entrusted and reported to them by the Mfumu-mbôngi, the community president. Such problems are delegated to community leaders by the Mbôngi or the Fôngo of Mbôngi in accordance to the needs relative to the problem and the surrounding policy. The ministers of Mfûndu hold the same authority and the same rights towards duties in each of their "ministerium." If one considers the concept of hierarchy which is invading the African world today, these "Zimbuta" (wise and powerful elders) would be entitled "ministers without portfolio" within the government of Mbôngi. And it is the type of position which holds the key to why corruptibility is almost non-existent within the administrative organization of the collective policy of the Mbôngi.

Each "Nkutu," or portfolio, in this political system (of Mbôngi) is the responsibility not of a sole individual (Dingizi/Sièlo or minister), but of a whole group of individuals according to community testimonies about their deeds concerning the Mbôngi and the community. It is the responsibility of each elected Mfûndu to establish its agenda and its schedules. Once the Mfûndu is seated, its official members cease to see themselves as individuals in order to act as a united body in conformity to the community constitutional right entrusted in them.

Within the community as well as within the country the Mfûndu of Mbôngi are numerous and diverse. They increase in number according to the cultivation of the knowledge and technological skill within the community. New knowledge and technologies within a community often call for new types of Mfûndu (commission). Although Mfûndu are numerous and diverse, we can classify new and existing forms under two main groups: The public Mfûndu and the Mfûndu à *huis clos*.

When the public Mfûndu take place, in an open court or inside a cabinet, interested people can be seated in its bosom and follow the debates as auditors and observers without taking any active part. Mfûndu à huis clos (Mfûndu zanswèki/ Mfûndu za kingenga/ Mfûnda za ku nim'a vitu) are not open to the public; only primary members of these Mfûndu have a seat at their bosom. Such Mfûndu or commissions can take place inside the village or outside of it under the form of "Wûbi" (a business meeting) which, very often, are held under the shadow of a tree within a savannah, or on a "Lônde," the top of a hill or plateau. These particular Mfûndu meet privately to discuss the most serious problems raised by the community or communities—or often meet in this style just to plan certain projects or actions to be undertaken within the community or between communities and regions.

In old times, most Mfûndu were organized around the following issues relating to political, educational, cultural, economic, and technological realities of the time:

1. Market, trade, laws, governments, and money
2. Food gathering, fishing and hunting
3. Marriage (alliances) and diplomacy
4. Pottery, weaving and forging (industries)
5. Death: funerals, mummifications and banquests
6. Education: initiation, specialization and handicrafts
7. Health and medicine
8. Justice and tribunal
9. Migration (settlements in new sites)
10. Choice of chiefs
11. Quarrels and wars
12. Social and political organization
13. Contact with alien people
14. Work and rewards
15. Beliefs: myths, ancestors, spirits, "gods," life
16. *Adopting* new community members [23b]

Due to the continual development of community knowledge and experience, these questions and issues are no longer treated today in the same manner as the past because people have acquired a new insight on them. Mfundu themselves have been structurally improved. Each Bântu subculture has developed types of specialization concerning the art of organization in social affairs. The use of symbols as ways of representing and interpreting information has been developed although it was not practiced by every community member. Political knowledge, the key to social organization, has also developed. And with this gradual development in organizational knowledge and social technology, the government of Mbôngi and its constitution have also improved. A new policy which concentrates on social problems was born. With this, a new and fundamentally *collective policy* of Mbôngi government, a new system, antagonistic towards corruptibility and community corruption, was also born. The concept of Mfûndu was developed—new responsibilities and new organization were introduced into the government of the community Mbôngi. Certain Mfûndu became specialized and held special responsibilities within the community. New forms of Mfûndu were introduced and many older improved. Divisions of responsibilities in Mfûndu became distinct and clear. Individual responsibilities and duties towards oneself, one's family, and one's community were regularized and precisely defined. Though community policy, the capacity to discuss questions that could arise in the Mfûndu was developed. Such matters, among others, include:

1. All questions related to community lands and boundaries (including their inalienability);
2. Economic issues: trade, cooperatives, markets, work, money;
3. Education of community youth (including new types of initiation);
4. Community and the country's policy within and towards the community;
5. Industries: forging, weaving, pottery, brewery;
6. Ranching;
7. Authorities;
8. Alien people and the community;
9. Knowledge and science;
10. Physical and intellectual development (exercise, dance, games, etc.);
11. Routes (roads) and transportation;
12. Cultures and languages;
13. Marriage and the community (alliances/diplomacy);
14. New techniques (in art, weaving, etc.);
15. Government and community members;
16. Health, medicine, death;
17. Construction;
18. Town and village life;
19. Army and security;
20. Travel and transport;
21. History and culture;
22. Wars and revolutions.

The Mfûndu, although ignored by the political organization of modern African governments, is a well known, well respected, and well received political organization by the majority of African Bântu people in their rural milieu where it is practiced on a daily basis. It is a system deep-rooted in an authentic foundation of "Kisinsi," the system of African reality (with all its faults and its qualities) and African people want and accept it into their local reality.

Modern African governments today would be rooted in full security if they would only search for their foundations within ancient political institutions such as the community Mbôngi, the most stable among African institutions still existing. It is in this *denial* of Mbôngi wherein lies the source of political and social complications and disorders into which the African world is driven today. Modern African governments lead their people under radically new systems, alien to Africa, while the people themselves and *their* community organizations live by other systems. The community systems, very old and deeply rooted in their concepts, are systems which respond to the socio-political and economic African reality, the "Kisinsi" or "Kisafelika." Such local African systems, hated by regimes implanted into modern Africa, were soon baptized "backward," "illogical," "not intelligible and non-scientific by the imperialistic, violent, and murderous "civilizations" based upon Western science and technology. But one must be convinced that without the survival of the well-integrated practices of these "uncivilized" and "non-nuclearing" traditional African systems, many modern nations in present day Africa would have, after decolonization, lost more than half of their populations. At this point in time a loaf of bread is worth over $10.00 in certain African cities and corruption has become "legal currency." This state of corruptibility is impossible in the administrative organizatin of the Mbôngi government.

It is very difficult to corrupt a member of Mfûndu because of his political and cosmological world view, unintelligible and mysterious not only to the alien of the "scientific" and "technological" world, but even to modern African leaders who, gropingly, are seeking to impose upon their nations systems unfit for African realities. Through the policy of Mbôngi, members of Mfûndu commissions retain their forces of resistance against corruptibility.

Corruptibility among the Bântu has always been considered a criminal act of a great danger by all members of the Mbôngi government. If authoritative members of Mfûndu (appointed members) had been corrupted through accepting illicit payments in order to cover up truth, such authorities were obliged to accept the consequences of decisions by the Mbôngi against them and their wrong doing. These consequences could be payment of correctional fine, exile through "sell" or, in certain cases, live burial in the market place (Kunwa kimbokoto). Sometimes corrupted members were psychosomatically tortured by the public—the community would stay aloof from them, point at them, and laugh at their sight. There was no defense for such individuals in the community legal system.

This collective policy by the Mbôngi is a system which first of all thinks of the community and its members. Protecting and insuring its life within the social standards (according to the conditions of life in a given period of time) are its first responsibilities. The policy of this system, on the other hand, also possesses a very high degree of humanism regarding all "aliens" without any consideration of skin pigmentation or national origin. This was not understood by the West when its colonists were penetrating continental Africa. We will come back to this point later.

When agents of exploitation and the imperialistic principle shout "Freedom and democracy at home" [while exporting chaos abroad], leaders of the violently impoverished nations of Africa (voluntarily ignoring misery, sickness and strange forms of deaths introduced by the imperialist/capitalists), shout out in a "new African humanistic style: "Welcome to Africa, the continent of legendary hospitality. The continent where nations offer their guests of 'marque' not wine, food or corrupting speeches (as do our hosts in the West) but lands, elephant tusks, gold and diamonds in enormous quantities." Despite the very devastating economic and financial situation of his country, and fully knowledgeable of the effect of famine on his people, Bokassa did not hesitate to offer to the French president, Giscard D'Estang, a preserve of hunting land of 3,000 square miles in addition to the quantities of diamonds he gave him.[24] And Bokassa is not alone in such evil and criminal practices in Black Africa with its strange and blind modern policies. This type of blind hospitality had, in olden times, been formulated by many African despots who wanted alien military support in order to maintain their power for life. It was also this type of blind hospitality in which certain agents of exploitation were received in certain parts of Africa during its colonial penetration: food, transportation, women, and land were given freely for the colonists' basic needs, which are well understood by African people. But as reward for this "hospitality without measure," the beneficiaries of this hospitality, agents of exploitation, took their firearms and attacked their unarmed hosts. Africans were slaughtered mercilessly and their lands seized. Was not the overthrow of the "immortal emperor" Bokassa orchestrated by his own guests of 'marque' to whom he offered a portion of Centrafrican territory?

The point of such examples is this: for their blind humanism, African people were made slaves in their own home; with the same blindness, the whole of Black Africa is today suffering and its new leaders seem proud of it. They want to rule forever because their job has received an excellent "mark" from their masters who continue to teleguide them, saying "Go ahead and kill all your citizens and clear more room for us and our businesses. Money, tanks, and the like are all coming to support your good job." Many rulers in today's Africa are ruling not because they are aware of social and economic needs of their country, but because they have accepted to be instruments of the power of violence.

The hatred against foreigners which is germinating in Africa today seems to be something imported. This hatred did not have a place in the traditional African policy of its Mbôngi. It is a new doctrine introduced with the penetration of modern capitalist exploitation of man by man. And as it was once said far earlier, despite skin color differences, white men's penetration of Africa was considered by many African societies on the seashore as the return of the ancestors' spirit because white men were seen coming out of "Kalûnga," the ocean. The Kalûnga in many African cosmologies is a wall and a door between the physical/biological world and the spiritual world,[25] the world of ancestors' radiations (Fu-Kiau, 1969; 1980).

Is it not, considering the above African cosmological world view, a total failure in the efforts of human mutual understanding that the West could not make a true and unseparable friend of Africa? Is it not the West, which by its total misunderstanding of the African humanistic creed, introduced the most evil political system that ever existed on the earth, the racist political club of western prisoners' descendants who settled inside Azania?

The true friends of Africa should be recognized on the basis of their attitude vis-a-vis the evil club-government in Azania. One cannot pretend to be political friends with Black Africa while supporting the Afrikaners' political rule in South Africa, a political club which is presently laying the ground work for a racial war in continental Africa. Because of their political blindness many African leaders do not even "cough" about the situation, since they are puppet-rulers appointed and supported by nations which also support the racist system implanted in Azania.

The society which holds the understanding that human beings, of all varieties, are brothers and sisters, members of the same *human family,* should not be called inferior or savage. The African's hospitality as well as his humanism are legendary even in the literature of his enemies. The Westerner was always received as a brother/sister and a friend in Africa as well as a visitor willing to settle or to pass by. Conflicts, tensions and wars began between the African and Westerner the moment the latter ventured to impose his desires and system upon African natives in an attempt to change them. The Westerner came to destroy the African system and the fundamentally collective and humanistic policy of Mbôngi—the basic African institution of public counseling, hearing, and decision making. Whites who have migrated into Azania (many of whom are descendants of prisoners, exiled from their country of origin) primarily ignore the African concept of Mbôngi policy vis-a-vis white visitors or other aliens. What these "visitors" have introduced to the Azanian community and the continent as well will sooner or later, through peace or war, change. And this, to use Morlan's expression, is because such whites "are not saints, but sinners who transgress the law of God and suffer [and will continue to suffer] for it."[26] One must know that these "sinners" ignore the fact that they are piloting a sinking boat destined for nowhere.

The politics of the community Mbôngi will reappear for the well being of the community and the country as well—this time, at the national level. It will reappear for the development and for the protection of all African inhabitants, indigenous or migrated, under the "Kisinsi," the most accepted African local system, with the assistance and collaboration of all Africans

Ian Smith (former rebel in Zimbabwe) is not yet dead. The change he used to hate in his all white, racist, and rebellious minority government, has already happened; whereas, his political and racist statements purported that change would only be possible in one thousand years, so far away after his death and that of all his grandsons. in other words, after the total impoverishment of the total exploitation of Zimbabwean people and their lands.

Unfortunately for Mr. Smith, we were not able to start "counting" those thousand long years—the "rain" that he meant by all means to prevent is now falling. Rhodesia suddenly became Zimbabwe, a nation facing towards the "Kisinsi"—the system based on the local African aspect of "Kibântu," the Bântu philosophy called "Huhuism/Ubuntuism" respectively of "Hunhu" (in Shona language) and of "ubuntu" (in Ndebele).

Today, Smith, the declared enemy of all Zimbabwean Blacks, became a full member of that same society search of its power and of its security which should have its foundation not outside of Zimbabwean concepts but within its own local political and philosophical system, its "Ubuntuism"—the Zimbabwean aspect of "Kibântu/Kibumûntu," the Bântu philosophy that Smith wanted dead and the philosophy that the Bântu transfer through their Mbôngi. Without this freedom deep in the Mbôngi concept in Zimbabwe, Smith will continue to be known as "Foreigner" in Zimbabwe no matter what was his power and his position in the alien minority government in which he was the "gang-master."

It is this "Ubuntu/Hungu" concept which generated the politics of Zimbabwean Mbôngi during the whole period of oppression. Smith, the "chauffeur," drove bombs into all Zimbabwean villages in order to destroy the people's Mbôngi, the Zimbabwean traditional political institution where the fate of Smith's minority rebellious government was at stake. Likewise, the South African white will never be accepted as full member of Azanian community unless he returns to reason as a human being in a world of cultural and social diversity and is ready to accept this simple, natural, and historical reality: that he is minority and immigrant, not a local but an international; and that he cannot be treated otherwise. it is his *duty* to change and, in cooperation with native Azanians, build an Azanian system which will please all Azanians and into which he will find his place as a full citizen.

I believe new African governments can still be born today which will take into consideration the traditional political organization of the Mbôngi system and with their birth, new forms and aspects of Mbôngi-type governments adaptable to the time in which we all live. They will be governments taking seriously into consideration the basic human needs of their communities for the betterment of those who live there—*not* community consideration based upon members' origin, skin or native tongue.

CHAPTER V
THE KISINSI SYSTEM

Every individual of this planet on which we live is a citizen of the planet. He has the right to join any "Kânda" (community, race, society) of his choice and live in any social environment if he is ready to respect the systems prevailing within the organizational structure of that "Kânda." If he or she is an immigrant to that community or society, it is his or her duty to adapt him/herself to the systems of that society and new geographical milieu. Acting contrary to this principle often brings about disastrous consequences. "Ku nsi angana nata nôngo (yilôndanga), kunat'ândi kibâku ko (kibâkanga)" a Kôngo proverb states: "In an alien country, take a needle with you (that which mends and pieces together), but do not take a "Bâku" knife (that which tears and destroys)."

Without doubt, Africa is far ahead with regard to the question of humanistic and racial relationships. One may even be tempted to say that blacks were once blind to skin color. When an alien did respect his own visitor's status without attempting to convert or alter the African "Kisinsi" (the local system), he was welcomed as a member of the family—because as part of the human family, "If by your labor you feed the 'Tûtu' (rat of the city), you also have to feed the 'Mbènde' (rat of bush) because the latter is a runner" (Kôngo proverb). The moral of this proverb is to respect "runners"—travelers or alien people—because they can build or destroy your home.

In the Western world, what is often done is first to prevent aliens access to work, even if they are able. By preventing access to work, aliens are "taught" to pursue lying, corruption, and, often, how to become terrorists. It is not surprising that most embezzlements in the Third World Countries are made by those who had been brainwashed in the western world—where unlike the African concept, the access to work is not seen as a fundamental human right but as an irrational discriminatory system of human "survival."

The alien that you welcome today under your roof can be the political leader of his country tomorrow. your welcome to him can convey and even influence his policy vis-a-vis the world in general and vis-a-vis your country in particular. On the contrary, hatred towards an alien can hurt both the world and your country, for aliens are often "Mbènde malwalumuka" (the runner rats, Mbènde), i.e. travelers and "breakers" of news.

According to the policy of the Mbôngi, all aliens entering the community or the country (region) were classified in three main groups, and each of them had the right to that *first and fundamental African human right—access to work* in order to provide one's daily bread. Each category had its "corner" or its place within the constitution of the Mbôngi. These categories are as follows:

a/ *The "N'nânga."*

A "N'nânga" is an individual "bought" by the community. To "be bought" means to be accepted as a full community members in a lineage into which one is not a blood-related member. This was a traditional African way of officially adopting new members (young and old, but never children) into the community. Hence, when an alien individual arrives within the community, he is allowed total freedom as an independent human being in all his activities. He was never seen or considered a "beast of burden" as in the case of slavery within Europe and the New World. In the community of Mbôngi, this originally "bought" or "adopted" individual could cultivate and harvest the land of his new community with full rights. He could have a family and take care of it according to social standards of life style. He had rights and liberty to everything within the community, although he could take the leadership of the community policy only according to certain circumstances.

As long as the community had its own original "Nkasi/Lesi" (heroes/militants) be they male or female able to take direction of the community leadership, the access to that position was prohibited to community "adopted" members. In the case where the community lacked the person able to lead the community, then the "N'nânga" or the adoptee could temporarily assume that responsibility of head of the Mbôngi—until the time when the community again had its own hero of full community blood to reassume such responsibility.

Although the N'nânga was a full member of the community, he could not change his original "Luvila" (ethnic link identification, as praise name) or his "Ndumbudulu" (ethnic motto identification, as community standing). These symbolize his regional or national ethnic identity, his true historico-biologic citizenship roots.

When a female N'nânga or alien had offspring after her community integration, her children were known as the "kids-result-of-community-wealth." Such children became full community members although their biological origin came from a woman of different "Luvila" (ethno-biologic link). Such children, however, were not known like this if the father was a member of the local indigenous community. In this case, the children were very often adopted for "Luvila" and for "Ndumbudulu"—those of the community integrated by their mother. But they could also keep their mother's previous community status. I rather prefer to use "adoptees" and "adopters" than slaves and masters in African practice of the so-called "slavery," since the concept of slavery based on the "slave-master" relationship of the West did not exist in Africa. In practice, there was no difference between "slave" and "master" in Mbôngi.

b/ The "Minyisila"

The "Minyisila" are individuals voluntarily leaving their region (territory), country, community or race in order to settle down in an area or community of their choice. The term "Minyisila" itself stems from the verbal root "Yisa" (to come) which, in its turn, gives "Yisila" (to come for) expressing intentions contained in the "Yisa" action taken by the "N'yisila" (singular of Minyisila).

One distinguishes the following subgroups among "Minyisila": A) The N'natuki" or alien who arrives with a desire to settle down, work or even to hide himself. B) The "Kwângi" or stranger entering the com-munity/country to escape some situation that can be a natural pheno-mena (drought), political/ideologic reason (war) or social and psycholo-gical reasons (need of family). Therefore "Minyisila" as a group are refugees, or individually, honest migrants or exiled or escaping prisoners. The "Kwângi/Bikwângi" term constitutes a larger group of alien entering a region/country at once, mainly for political reasons. These are also classified as "refugees."

c/ The N'zièti

All alien individuals visiting the country for a short period of time and who desire to leave the country after that period are known as N'zièti or Nzènza. According to the African political concept described here, such an alien cannot change his alien status into the status of local Kisinsi, his newly adopted system.

Every foreigner has the freedom of settling in most communities under the protection of laws and rights of the community where he or she holds his historic or biological link. Despite these rights, however, an alien in Africa was not warranted "Kisinsi," the historical right of natural citizenship. If the individual resides in the community or the country for a long period of time, one simply says that he became "Nkièvo mwisinsi," an "indigenous-like person" or "citizen-like." This is a way of stating that the individual is a "pseudo-citizen," an element always between lines—a man on the margin. "If the alien warrants the status of Kisinsi," a Kôngo proverb says, "he can bungle everything; he is even able to wipe out the 'Kânda' (race/community) for his own interest."

The foreigner within the community, according to the Mbôngi political system, remains a foreigner. The community, in any circumstance, cannot change his label of alien and his origin in "Kisinsi." The sole and greatest responsibility of the community or country towards an alien is to keep him. He provides his own food and shelter through work, as if he were a member of right and of blood within the community—as long as he does not strike out upon the systems of the country and that community in which he lives.

In the past, the community used to grant every alien the right to cultivate and harvest the community land as well as the right to use and sell what was produced while living as alien within the community/country. He was also allowed to forge and practice the art of pottery—but could not exploit a mine of clay or copper without a special permit of agreement with the country by the Mbôngi government of the community in which the landlord of the mine is involved. As previously mentioned, if a male alien was married to a sister of the community or country, his children became full members of the community. If he married outside the community (country), his children (as he himself), are strangers and immigrants within the community. The community/ country system will not change such aliens' original "Kisinsi" and their state of being "strangers."

For the Bântu people and the Kôngo in particular, the Kisinsi is not something out of convention; one sees it as natural and unchangeable. Anywhere he may be, the Mûntu (singular of Bântu) is member of the community or country where he originated (his "Fuma—stump) and where the "M'fuma" (baobob), the natural and spiritual symbolic landmark, was erected as a symbol of "Kimfumu" (chiefdom and authority) and of his "Mfumu" (chief/leader). All this can be held as fundamentally real or as purely symbolic within the collectively cosmologic experience of the community/society. A Mukôngo person can, for example, become a Canadian; with this new status one will say of him, according to the concept of Kisinsi described here, that the "Kisikanada" or "Kimwisikanada" he adopts is only a "political" cloth while his "Kisikôngo," ceremonially broken, remains his natural and unchangeable "Kisinsi" because it has a biological link. The "Kisinsi," for the Bântu and Kôngo in particular, is not obtained by any ceremony—"Diâmbu diamena ye diambutukila" (It is a naturally grown matter). One has it in one's blood. It does not change by changing or adopting new environments. For the Bântu, naturalization is just a political game for survival, a cloth to be put on and to be taken off. With this cloth, spying agencies have today the power they have never had to penetrate institutions all over the world.

The community and its policy can be destroyed if they are both controlled by alien forces. Likewise, a country and its government can be pulled down and/or demolished if they are led by a policy whose roots lie in an imported system of thought, one which is perhaps opposed to local systems. Such a situation could be dangerous and devastating for the nation as a whole. And this has become a common situation in Third World countries; a disease that extends rapidly, like a poison devouring the people and their economies because their leaders have built "aside" practices of their own Mbôngi, the traditional African system's stamp of political identity.

CHAPTER VI
MBONGI AND ECONOMIC SYSTEMS

"Politics and economy (are) twins"—Kinzônzi ye Kimvwâma, nsîmba—says a Kôngo proverb. There is not one without the other.

Each society has its own concept of politics and economy based on its own world view, its concept of life, and its experience. No concept is better or worse. In their Mbôngi system political power among the Bântu is a shared power. Their system of economy, as is their political power, is a shared system. The institution of Mbôngi presented here has a clear distinction between what it calls "Kimvwâma kia tumba evo n'zo" (the economy of pyramids) and "Kimvwâma kiayalangana evo kia Nkat'a dingo-dingo" (the universal economy or the spiral economy).

A. *The 'pyramid' economy.*

The economy of "Tumba/N'zo," or the economy of pyramid/pile, is an individualistic economy because it accumulates itself in the hands of the few and for the needs of the few. This is the economy of the capitalistic type. This type of economy grows upwards and narrowly to what may be called the summit of "N'zo/Tumba," the pyramid's sharpest point of accumulation, or of progress/success. Once this sharpest point of accumulation is reached, the system very often creates all kinds of tensions within its market emvironment of consumers: political as well as economic crises, moral decline, corruption, social abuses, and/or terrorisms of all kinds which are all symptoms pointing to the fall of the system and development of new grounds and a new beginning. I call this type of economy a "nuclearing" or a dead-end system because of these characteristics. Its highest point of accumulation/profit, the sharpest point of progress, is always a sign of conflicts and wars between nations.

The Bântu, in their Mbôngi system of economy tend to avoid such a system, which they also call "Fu kia dûnga biambi," a system of unfortunate catastrophes/disasters: conflicts, insecurity, wars, massacres and the like. For the Bântu, the economy of "pyramids" is an economy that escapes its builders, those who should benefit from a social economy. The more wealth people accumulate in the "pyramids" of owners through various means of production, the less the share holders or beneficiaries have, and the more frustrated the producers become—because the economic growth of the system has become concentric and is vertically focused towards the few, the "proud." It is at the sharpest point of the pyramid (Tumba), as a matter of fact, that rebellions, strikes, and revolts become perpetual and certain to explode. The sake of new grounds for more pyramids and for more systematic killings (elsewhere for new market) become the fundamental results.

Within this economic system of "Tumba" (pyramids), all business profit goes "up" to the few, the owners of the means of oppression and production (fig. 6). For many, this economic system is the synonym to power. The crux of what is happening in Third World nations today, especially in Africa, is that this system is being introduced through shotgun force. With the concept that money equals all power, power equals superiority, and superiority equals all rights to save or to kill which is invading Africa, modern African leaders are emptying the trunks of the commonwealth for their sake of power to become even richer than the capitalists themselves—this, in order to *hold* the power that they "need." Here again, these leaders forget the wise Kôngo proverb "Mbôngo kavûmbulanga mfumu ândi ko (kânsi mûntu)"—Money never lifts its master from his bed of sickness, but a human being can.

Goods are means; they are not power. Only man, as a "second sun" radiating around the world through his deeds, is power. "Bôle, bôle; bukaka, n'sôngo" (literally "Two is two; loneliness is a disease") says another Kôngo proverb. Real power is something to be shared and to be proud of. A collectively shared political power within the community/country is the political power that lasts. To practice "togetherness" (Kibôlebôle/duality or collectivism), sharing the happiness of social, political and economic life, can make everything possible to a community/country; but the egotistic loneliness that builds economic pyramids for the few kills because it is a disease. This pseudo-power of the few is a "nuclearing" power that destroys not only life, but can also blow up the planet on which we live.

B. *The 'Horizontally-Spiral' Economy.*

The second type of economic system that the Mbôngi policy identifies is what is called "Kimvwâma kia nkat'a dingo-dingo," the horizontally spiral economy "vital roll." This is an economy that "ties," touches and satisfies all social strata of the system. The Bântu themselves, in general, and the Kôngo in particular, see this type of economy as a *perpetual* system. It is an economy based upon life and not an economy of destruction. Because of its emphasis on life and change through "Dingo-

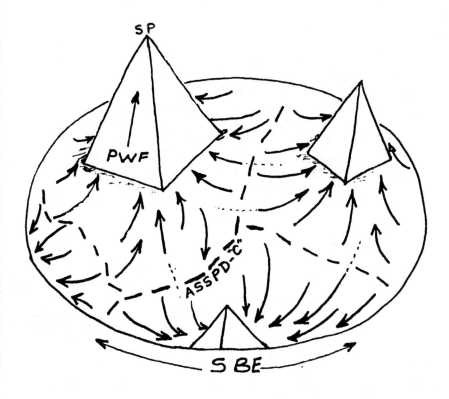

Fig. 6: Economy of pyramids or the system whose "goods" run away from the producers.

SBE   —the entire Social Body and its Environment are in service of the few, owners of means of oppression and production.

PWF   —Pyramids of Wealth for the Few (but collectively built by the social body in its own environment)

ASSPD-"C"—Apparent, Sectorial Social and Political Divisions (termed as) of Competition, source of many crimes, tensions and wars.

SP   —once the pyramids reach their "Sharpest Point," the system turns against their builders (lay off, service cuts).

    —the arrow indicates the motion of productive force.

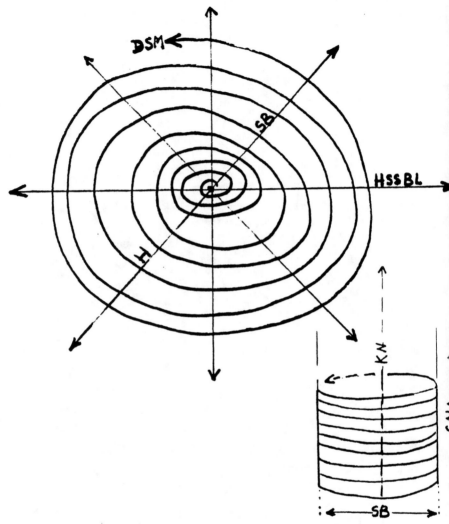

Fig. 7: Economy of "Nkat'a ngôngo" or the horizontally-spiral system.

DSM   —Direction of the Spiral Motion, the symbol of egalitarianism in the collective economy of Mbôngi.

H-SB   —the Horizontality indicates the Social Body which constitutes the productive power of the whole "Lukosi," the economic web.

HSSBL—the output (in Mbôngi system) is Horizontally Shared through all Social Body Layers (its producers).

CALA the Collectively Accepted Level of individual Accumulation or the cylinder of tolerated wealth (each house, for example, must have its "Nkânk'a nguba" or a standard, cylindrical basket of peanuts − ±3m³)—rural milieu.

KN   —"Kintombayulu kia Nsînsani" or the Competitive Verticality of mass-pollutes and leads to mass-killing is not tolerated in Mbôngi economy.

dingo" (the natural way of cosmic motion), it is also called "Fu kia môyo wa kimvwâma kiakôndwa nsukulu," an endless economic system of vitality.

Such an economic system is slow, sure and non-violent. It increases and expands in time and space through all social layers, but satisfies all the basic needs of its builders, the community members. The more people produce in this economy of "Nkat'a dingo-dingo," the more their share in it increases. Their lives are enjoyable and their vitality (shared force and power) increases because the economic growth of the system is horizontally eccentric while growing or moving up. The economic growth, like life (contrary to the economy of pyramid/"Tumba") has no end—in comparison to the sharpest point of accumulation and "no return" in the pyramid-economy.

The "Nkat'a dingo-dingo" economy does have its positive and negative sides. Its birth and renovation are perpetual and horizontally spiral. They both follow the notion of "N'kîngu a dingo-dingo," the spiral principle of life and change which also operates through people's lives in the cosmic living microcosms (fig. 7). Such an economy also represents a solid and coherent "body" in form of "N'suma,"[27] the cylinder/prism of wealth (known also in Kikôngo as "Nkânk'a mvwîlu."

The "Nkata dingo-dingo" economy is a well patterned system, covering everything under its umbrella including the community and all its members. There is no landlord in the Mbôngi system of economy, but only the "Kânda"—the whole community. The land, source of life and happiness, belongs to the community. The chief of the land is only the *manager* of community affairs and properties, not a "land lord." The rights to the use of the community lands belong to all, no matter what their individual status. No individual, even the chief, has the right to sell an inch of community land. Yet the Kânda economic system does not experience catastrophic crises because its economy symbolizes life motion itself—which is a key concept in the Bântu world view and belief. The economy is an endless system with no concept of "sharpest point" of development which eventually leads to nuclearing or self-destructive power—as does the pyramid-economy.

One can see that the horizontally spiral economic system is deeply rooted with the Bântu's world view, their cosmologies[28] which regenerates it as well. The Kôngo say "Mbôngi a kânda ka yitûngwanga va lwèka lwa fu kia kânda ko:" the community, substructural, political institution of Mbôngi is not built *aside* the system of the community/society and its world view (proverbs 2.7 and 2.8). The concept of the social life of a people, its world view, and its system of economy are one. A nation or a society suffers critically only if its world view and its system of economy are in conflict or contradiction. This is when they no longer are one.

The people of Africa and the many political systems imposed on them are suffering today because these new systems are diametrically opposed to their concept of life and of collective economy. Because of this, new African institutions suffer. If one wants to cure the ailing continent politically, philosophically and economically, such apeing or "wax-behavior" must change. The African Bântu economy based upon a collective and shared economy, as it remains in the rural milieu, could be used as a modern model to change this situation today, and the chaos of economic and community contradiction could possibly be brought into harmony.

CHAPTER VII
A WORD OF CONCLUSION

This short study on the Bântu people's political concept of Mbôngi may not be an exhaustive one; but I have attempted to speak about an important African traditional institution through the perspective of stressing the need for modern African leaders to look to the Mbôngi system as a wise and well-developed role-model for both an African system of economy and political organization. This is the Mbôngi's value as a basic institution of politics in Bântu countries such as Angola, Azania, Burundi, Congo, Namibia, Tanzania, Zaire, and Zimbabwe, to name only a few.

The concept of Mbôngi discussed within can be a key to studies that other young African scholars might undertake in search of African political systems—studies necessary to point out paths towards saving the African world which has become the prisoner of rebellion, corruption, exploitation, famine, disease, and unusual death.

As a system of viable political organization, the Mbôngi (in its present state) belongs on the bottom rung of political organization in the modern Bântu states, the powerless level of the masses. Its concept as a basic African political and economic system is only understood by those who do not have political or economic power or control at the national level. These are the poor villagers who have become perpetual prey to the exploitation of imported systems. Such people are prisoners of modern African dictatorships today; dictators supported by the international, imperialistic financial clubs of the world.

Yet despite all this, the village or community Mbôngi remains one of the unique symbols of the types of ancient political institutions which have survived the oppression of imported systems. If this institution has survived before and after times of colonization, we have good reason to conclude that the foundation of African future can also be built upon the basis of the solid principles of the Mbôngi institution. Rethought and improved, such institutional role models can aid in shaping Africa to *be* African in politics, economy and community.

Many states, kingdoms and empires known in the Africa of the past exist only in books or in name today, but the Mbôngi and its coherent political organization still remains. Its politics and responsabilities vis-à-vis the communities and their members are held in more respect by Africans than many modern governments led by despotic African technocrats corrupt to the tip of their tongues. In communities where the Mbôngi government arranges and discusses all, people may remain poor, but they are *equal*—never poor or rich in sharp inequalities. Levels of economic division such as "poor" and "rich" do not exist in the practice of Mbôngi policy, though rich as well as poor may exist at a certain level within the community.

The present "Mal" (illness) of many Black Africa systems of economy is a modern political creation by those in power. It is the result of unfit systems adopted (often through imposition, of course) by political leaders. The latter are often under pressure from external systems because they opted to build their nations' politico-economic systems "aside" local politico-economic substructural realities. But such leaders have ignored their African roots of *collective* economy for collective life and happiness.

*

* *

I will conclude with a note about an experience I myself have witnessed in my home region of Kivûnda, Luôzi (Lower Zaire).

One day my assistant and I took a dirt road towards a village where I had an appointment with a "Ngânga-n'kisi," a specialist in traditional medicine. Unfortunately, we had our shoes on. Once we arrived in the village, the wife of the Ngânga shouted out at the sight of us: "You passed my husband at his 'brewery.' But it does not matter; take seats and let's wait for him." We each took a "Kikulu" (literally the stool on which one sits to tell and transfer the past, the history) and waited.

After a few hours of waiting, we saw the Ngânga-n'kisi coming from the village exit. A calabash of "Nsâmba" (vegetal milk/wine) was dangling down his back from his left shoulder and he was murmering as he walked gnashing his teeth . . .

Upon approaching the door of his house, he put down his sack and the calabash containing the vegetal milk (served as a wine) and said to us: "Batâta (Sirs): because you have accepted to wear shoes, no longer can one communicate with you by your feet. You just passed me at my brewery (Sokolo)!"

* *

*

The old man, the barefoot specialist in the story above, was not jealous to see young people wearing shoes (he himself wears them occasionally on special days). Knowing that I was someone interested in our past and its value in modern Africa, he simply wanted to offer a lesson that by stripping oneself of all one's "Kisinsi," one's cultural identity, one can "tangle oneself up" complete. This is to call for ignorance and disorder in the country. According to the Ngânga-n'kisi's traditional ideas, based upon knowledge passed on by the Kisinsi concerning "waves and radiations" in the process of communicating information, I should have been warned by stumble if I had walked that distance barefooted.[28b]

For a true African, the foot serves as a receptor, a physical or body antenna (Mwèkese) and alerts one of the arrival of radiations / waves of communication. Even if one stumbles with shoes, explains the concept, it is not easy to receive information in order to interpret the message contained in the "communication" of radiations received. "A borrowed wrap does not allow one to dance at one's ease," a Kôngo proverb says. Whoever wants to play political games and dances well in political "dances" inside one's society, knows that there are political "wraps" that fit well in various political dances inside one's community / society: developed cultural understanding, use of the language or languages of the people, building upon conceptual reality of the society, sharing the community life style, etc. These are the most common and most powerful wraps which fit well, and whoever wants to join political "dances" must learn to wear them at the appropriate time not to exploit but to serve better the community / society and its systems.

An "African authority" must necessarily learn, first of all, to code and decode social, political or economic questions and problems on the grounds of African substructural systems. He or she will then be able to know, through the help of his own society, how to "tie" (code) and "untie" (decode) questions and problems arising in other systems only slightly known or entirely unknown to him (reason for the existence of advisors in all Mbôngi institutions).

To understand African systems, one must know that governing, like surviving, is learning to "tie" (code) and "untie" (decode) the knots or codes of systems and "radiations" through the world in which we live.[29] This coding and decoding process must start at home, with our environment, and at the seat of our own government. Whoever can succeed in this process can win full political support of the people he wants to lead.

The study of Mbôngi politics and its system of organization can provide a new insight into the organization of African modern higher institutions which are laying the foundations of African political systems. Mfûndu commissions, for example, can be used as role models for national institutions or special commissions of research and planning (on special questions) linked to ministerial cabinets. Such national commissions could hold the following responsibilities, according to ministerial cabinet function:

1. The detection of inter-ethnic cultural and social structural differences throughout the nation. The factors that unite or separate them politically, philosophically, economically, and conceptually. Such a basic and fundamental work could be of great aid to those called upon to serve the nation, in areas of legislation, justice, etc.

2. The study of regional as well as national needs to assist national planning teams in matters of projects to be implemented in given areas.

3. The study of ways and means needed to facilitate social and cultural contacts between different regions of the country. The investigation of existing contacts and their location and networks.

4. The printing and diffusing in African national languages of results of national studies. This could, undoubtedly, build national unity upon the grounds of its own general culture.

5. The organization of regional mobile cultural centers led by individuals creating and facilitating national development through study of African political, economic and philosohical aspects of life.

6. The submission to African governments and institutions of general recommendations eliciting the will of citizens concerning:
—national policy and government
—community and economy
—responsibilities in the process of nation building
—the army and the people
—national languages and political responsibilities for their use and preservation
—agriculture and national security
—constituency and voting issues
—human rights

To be African, Africa must necessarily stand upon foundations of its own reworked and reclaimed systems. Such foundations are not yet totally destroyed. The present study on Mbôngi is proof that existing traditional institutions *can* serve as role models today. It is a responsibility of young scholars to "dig up" these cultural treasures from their local cultures, which are littered and moulding inside the mud and sand of our own cultural unawareness.

The policy of urbanization adopted by many governments in Africa will not help to unearth these treasures which could lay down the foundation for the future of Africa and its political and economic position in the world. To satisfy the basic needs of African masses, it is imperative to *"ruralize"* African cities in order to *"urbanize"* the countryside. The luxuries of our generation—a generation that should be based upon true

African national liberation in all of its words and deeds—is nothing more than madness and a crime towards our societies, now perishing under systems that we have imposed upon them. To know and to respect our own African social and economic concepts is the first weapon against imported corruption in our countries. It is the knowledge and respect of our traditions that will also teach African people the qualities of the true leadership so needed in Africa today. The morally ill systems of the West, because of their "nuclearing" (mass killing) philosophy, will not help Africa to overcome its "mal."

The African Mûntu (person), because of his concept of respect and the value of a human being, insists, wherever he may be and whatever his strengths or weaknesses, that through the teaching of Mbôngi, all education must maintain community social values. Such maintenance is assisted by "Ndumbudulu" a process defined as continual interpretation and instructions by severe community self-criticism for new adaptations. As a conceptual term, Ndumbudulu derives from the verbal root "Lûmbula." The latter signifies "Enseigner (et) instruire três exactement"—To teach and to instruct very exactly.[30]

Lûmbula means also to erect fences, to limit or define exactly what a society wants to transfer to future generations about conceptual positions on the questions and problems of life. Lûmbula is to find ways and means by which community teaching and its culture can be transferred in a very exact manner according to social norms and values. Lûmbula is to form governments that should work for the community and its members, the strongest in the community as well as the weakest. It is to continue an education that should be inspired/regenerated by a policy whose roots are grounded in the foundation of solid African institutions such as the Mbôngi.

In order to build, one needs a foundation. Where there is no foundation, one cannot build. Africa is not building today because its modern leaders have lost the insight of their own foundation. Africa will never be African if it cannot build its proper foundation on its experience of the past—its immediate experience, opening the door to the *mediate* experience. Its traditional institutions and their systems are the foundation upon which modern Africa must *very carefully* build its future. African people, and especially African leaders, must prepare themselves to learn to listen and accept constructive criticism; for "Bitôdi n'lôndi" (says a Kôngo proverb)—criticism restores.

Let this study on Mbôngi and its political organization be for every African man and woman (and especially leaders of present African policy and those with the desire to know more about Africa and its people) a means of perpetuating African values and concepts about life and economy. Each system in the world economy is good in its social context. But what is good for one culture is not necessarily good for another culture. The worst mistake one person could make about the world's systems of economy is the attempt to blindly impose a system of economy upon another system under the pretext of being "scientific" and developed in a "higher" civilization. History has proven that sooner or later invading systems of economy will be violently blown up by the indigenous or "non-scientific" system—for societies, like human beings, prefer to grow in their own ways with very little external influence or pressure. What we have discussed within is that Africa is faced with a period of contradictions; nothing seems to be working because its people are rebelling against unfit or non-appropriate systems of economy and governance imposed upon them. Through this study, we think Black Africa may, through the model of Mbôngi community, rediscover the road to their "missing links" and shout *"Eureka!"* Without such a discovery, humanistically-based Africa will transform itself into a society without soul scoffing at the monumental Human Rights. African people as well as leaders must rethink themselves. The West as well as the East have no interest in developing Africa, only pure and simple exploitation of its people and of its resources. This situation must change!

The politics of the community Mbôngi will reappear, for the development as well as for the protection of all African inhabitants (indigenous or migrated), under the full power of the "Kisinsi" with the assistance and the collaboration of all Africans. Hence, I see returning to the African tradition of community-based Mbôngi as the first step in rethinking our traditions—basing the *future* on proven institutions of the African past and present.

FOOTNOTES

1. Coined word from four Kôngo words:*Nsi-Kânda-Ndînga-Lutèmoko* (Nation-people-Language-Civilization) or the "Nsikandîlu principle."

2. a/ *Kinsikandîlu* from: *Kisinsi-Kânda-Ndînga-Lutèmoko* (a concept of cultural awareness)

   b/ *Kinsonsikandîlu* from: *Kinsô*mpi-(kia) *Nsi-Kânda-Ndînga* (ye)-*Lutèmoko* (the state of cultural alienation, acculturation).

3. Fu-Kiau, 1980: *African Book Without Title* (private publication)

4. In French "Comté."

5. McNally, R., *Road Atlas (USA)*; Rand McNally? Co.: NY; NY. 1973 p. 105.

6. The term "Mbôngi" has been generally translated "Hut" in English. But the *Concept* inherent in the term Mbôngi and its role is far from the physical architecture of Mbôngi generally described in western literature of Africa. The best translation of Mbôngi in English language is "Public-Council-House," "Popular-Court," "House-of-Debates," or "Community-Parliament."

6b. Nicolai, H., 1961: *Luozi: Géographie Régionale d'un Pays du Bas-Congo;* CEMUBAC, Bruxelles.

6c. Excerpt from a song in *N'kûnga mia Kintwâdi;* CEDI/Kinshasa; 1956.

7. The word "Nkâka" can be translated: as grand-parent, or cousin (son or daughter of the paternal aunt in a matrilineage system).

8. For more information about "Nkôndi," see R.F. Thompson: "The Grand Nkôndi" in *Bulletin of Detroit Institute of Arts,* Vol. 56, No. 4, 1978.

9. Not knowing the true role of this "Hut" (museum), the West proceeded to call it a "House of spirits," or "Burial place." See Laman: *Dictionnaire Kikôngo—Francais*; Librairie Falk fils, Bruxelles, 1936.

10. See note 8.

11. If community therapeutic means failed, it was also possible to "chase" the guilty from the community and "sell" him/her; i.e. "to adopt him/her" as a way to isolate him/her and to prevent any contact

with the original community. After a certain period of time, the individual or his offspring (in case of death) could be "ransomed" (Kûlwa) and return to reintegrate with the community. This coming back process after ransom is called "Nkulukulu" of verbs "Kûluka" and "Kûlwa," to be ransomed.

12. Turnbull, C.M.: *Man in Africa,* N.Y.: Anchor Press; 1976, p. 286.

13. Turnbull, op. cit.; P.xix.

14. After colonial liberation, African woman has not only discovered the schooling but also, male nonchalance concerning agriculture or landwork. This has had a negative impact on African economy. Men are still unaware of fulfilling the vital role that the African woman played in the past as primary feeder of the community.

15. For more information about the concept inherent in the term *Nkutu* see Van Wing in his *Etudes Bakongo*; Bruxelles, 1959 and Troesch, J.: "Le Nkutu du comte de Soyo" in *Aequatoria* Nr. 2; 24e Annee.

16. Of Yâla: to govern, to administer; to pull up; to dig up
 N'yâdi / N'gyâdi: governor, authority
 Luyâlu: government, administration; discipline
 Kiluyâlu: authority of n'yâdi
 Mayâla: imperial authority, a despote
Kimayâla: despotism, imperialism
 Mfumu-mayâla: emperor, authority-of-authorities
 Kimfumu-mayâla: empire, domain of Mfumu-mayâla
 Yâdulu: insignia of power
 Ngyâdulu: manner of governing, governance
 -Angyâdila: adj. relative to yâdila
 -Angyâla: adj. relative to yâla
 Yalakana: potential of Yâla
 Yâlwa: to be governed / colonized; to be disciplined

16b. Smollin, M.A.: "What is in store for world leaders" in *Horoscope,* issue of January, 1983.

16c. Anna Tomforde: "West-Germans mark Hitler's rise" in *The Boston Sunday Globe*, Vol. 223 Nr. 30, 1983.

17. According to African traditions a child wears a rope around his waist or N'sing'a luketo and another around his neck (N'sing'a laka). Sometimes these two ropes were united by a third, vertical one, on the back. These two ropes constitute "Mantantulu" if they are united by a third vertical. They are worn during the period of birth until the age of three and were used as instruments of measure. With them, the mother or the nurse could make sure that the child is growing normally in physical development (weight and height) and control of health. When the circle of ropes become "Mpolunga (saggy) the mother was sure that her child was losing "volume" (Vônga / Vîmbu) or weight (zitu / kilu). This was a sure "Dîmbu" (symptom) that something was wrong with the

child's health. On the contrary, when ropes become tight against the body (kala nakekete), it was a good sign; a sign that the child was healthy and had a normal growth; then the mother had to enlarge the size of ropes' circles (Zèzisa/soba tèso bia n'singa).

17b. The "Luvèmba," literally gray or white hair, is the symbol of the negative element which, through age, accumulates "itself" in a biological organism. The Bântu believe that this element (associated with luvèmba/mpèmba) is the number one factor of natural death. Fu-kiau: *Cosmogonie Kôngo;* ONRD (Zaire) and *African Book Without Title*, private publication (Cambridge), 1980.

18. In ritual and initiative ceremonies, the "Kala" is the symbol of black color. The word itself signifies "to be," but also "alive coal."

19. As a catalyser in diverse ceremonies and rituals, "Kala-zima" (charcoal) is mainly used in psychosomatic treatments and in certain mystical and magic practices.

19b. Cited in Fu-Kiau's *Makuku Matatu*, forthcoming publication; Uppsala University, Sweden.

20. "Mfumu-za-mfûndu" are also called "Sièlo-bia-mfûndu" ministers-of-mfûndu; authorities-of-mfûndu; specialists or masters-of-mfundu; witnesses-of-mfûndu or counselors.

21. This procedure is of great value in a world with less or without writing skill: the world of "oralism".

22. The "Bèndo kia Mfûndu" or "Kiânzala kia Mfûndu" is considered as a cabinet in work meeting. It is generally an open place arranged under a tree shadow.

23. The Kôngo expression "To consult/demand the ancestor" is a synonym for the English phrases "Let's investigate" or "Let's dig through the old documents." The human experience accumulated in oral and pictorial archives kept by memories of "griots" (story tellers) are held in highest esteem by the entire Mbôngi community.

23b. I prefer to use *"adopting new members"* rather than "buying slaves" for the western concept of slavery did not exist in Africa. What is called in Kikôngo language "Sûmba n'nânga" (to buy a slave), for example, was in reality an *official way* or process *of adopting* new members in a community. "N'nânga" or slaves inside Africa were actually *"adoptees"* of the community. One must also understand that the African concept of child adopting did only exist within the community, i.e. between related members—at the death of the mother, a child is *given* to a relative (aunt, cousin, or an in-law) to be raised (adopting in western terms). An African person would never, traditionally, adopt his/her child outside of the extended family; the concept is seen as an abominable, moral and psychological crime not only against the child but against the whole extended family as well.

24. *The Boston Globe,* 1981, Vol. 219, No. 129.

25. It is believed that whoever (connotating a spiritual being) emerges from the world below to the upper world through "Kalûnga" (ocean) becomes a physical being. By the same token, the unborn are considered spiritual beings until they emerge from Mpemba (the mother womb) through the Kalûnga of the genital channel.

26. Gail Morlan, "Michiner: Rewriting History," in *South Africa,* VI. XIV, No. 3, May/June 1981.

27. The terms "N'suma" and its synonym "N'sundu" are, in the Kikôngo language, both used for the term "cylinder" (N'suma wavindumuka/N'sundu wavindumuka) and "prism" (N'sum'a bikônko/N'sundu a bikônko).

28. For more information, see Fu-Kiau, K.B., *Cosmogonie Kôngo,* ONRD/Kinshasa (Zaire); 1980: *Op. cit.*

28b. Man of our society has learned many ways to explain all radiations bathing and sensitizing him. It is a question, here, of radiations received by his body antennas, such as the foot. If one stumbled with one of his feet, one must know what foot and what part of the foot: the headfoot, its stomach, its foot or its sides. If it is a question of toe, what toe, etc. When he is on possession of all these informative data, he can closely guess the reason of his stumble.

29. Fu-Kiau, 1980: Op. cit.

30. Laman, K.E., 1936: Op. cit.

28. For more information, see Fu-Kiau, K.B., *Cosmogonie Kôngo,* ONRD/Kinshasa (Zaire); 1980: *Op. cit.*

28B. Man of our society has learned many ways to explain all radiations bathing and sensitizing him. It is a question, here, of radiations received by his body antennas, such as the foot. If one stumbled with one of his feet, one must know what foot and what part of the foot: the headfoot, its stomach, its foot or its sides. If it is a question of toe, what toe, etc. When he is in possession of all these informative data, he can closely guess the reason of his stumble.

29. Fu-Kiau, 1980: *Op. cit.*

30. Laman, K.E., 1936: *Op. cit.* p. 432.

Order form for books by Fu-Kiau

___ copies of *Mbôngi: An African Traditional Political Institution* ($12.95each) $___

___ copies of *Self-Healing Power and Therapy: Old Teaching from Africa* ($14.95 each) $___

___ copies of *Kindezi: The Kôngo Art of Babysitting* ($11.95 each) $___

___ copies of *Simba Simbi: Hold Up That Which Holds You Up* ($8.00 each) $___

___ copies of *African Cosmology of the Bântu-Kôngo* ($20.00 each) $___

Shipping and handling $___
($3.00 for the first book and $1.00 for each additional book)

TOTAL Enclosed: $___

Ship to:
Name: _____

Address: _____

_____

Send a photocopy of this order form, along with your check or money order, payable to Afrikan Djeli, to:

Afrikan Djeli   P.O. Box 50130   Atlanta, GA   30302-0130

Or order online at www.AfrikanDjeli.com